SAMURAI SUSHI

SAMURAI SUSHI

A FIELD GUIDE TO IDENTIFYING AND APPRECIATING
THE WORLD'S MOST UNIQUE WRAPS, ROLLS, AND SASHIMI

Bobby Suetsugu

BARNES
&NOBLE
BOOKS
NEW YORK

This edition published by Barnes & Noble, Inc., by arrangement with becker&mayer!

2005 Barnes & Noble Books

Copyright © 2005 by Bobby Suetsugu

ISBN: 0-7607-5933-2

M 10 9 8 7 6 5 4 3 2 1

Library of Congress Catalog-in-Publication data is available.

Design: Kasey Clark
Image Research: Shayna Ian
Editorial: Conor Risch
Production Coordination: Leah Finger
Project Management: Sheila Kamuda

Photographs by Keith Megay

Illustrations courtesy of NOAA Fisheries

Printed in China

I dedicate this book to my mother, Betty Etsuko Suetsugu

Contents

Introduction
The Making of a "Sushiman"

··

In December 1959, I was born in Seattle to parents who had both immigrated to America from Japan. I grew up much like any other American boy, but parts of my life were uniquely Japanese. One aspect of my heritage in particular would change my life.

I began practicing the Japanese sport of judo at the age of five and continued it for the next ten years. When I was fifteen, after my first year of high school, my judo instructor, Mr. Yukia Ninomiya, presented me with the opportunity to go to Japan for the summer to learn about sumo wrestling. I took this chance and spent the next ten years of my life there training and competing as a sumo wrestler.

The experience of being a sumo wrestler in Japan was incredible. It is said in Japan that sumo wrestlers are godly figures who bring good luck, health, and fortune to those who are near them. I was treated like a king.

At twenty-five I began speaking with my stable master about the next life, about what I was going to do after sumo—like any professional sport, a career in sumo can only last so long. He suggested sushi, and helped me find a position as an apprentice in the *sushi-ya* (sushi shop) of one of our sponsors.

I trained for one year under master chef Yoshio Takasaki, and he taught me almost everything I know about sushi. I was then given the opportunity to go to Hokkaido and begin working as a sushi chef for two brothers who owned a restaurant there.

I spent two years working in Hokkaido, practicing what I had learned and continuing my education. Every day the brothers had me cutting fish. The most important ability for a sushi chef is using a knife, and after two years cutting fish nearly every day, my knife skills were excellent. The knife became part of my hand.

While I was in Hokkaido I decided that I wanted to return to the United States. I took an opportunity to go back to Tokyo to spend another year there working and completing my training.

On returning to America in 1989, I worked in two New York City sushi restaurants, and later returned to Seattle, where I opened my own place: Sushiman.

One of the most rewarding things about owning a *sushi-ya* is introducing something special to my customers.

As the pace of the world increases, we're losing the love that comes from food—the act of eating and sharing with family and friends. It has become increasingly hard for us to sit down and share a meal with the people close to us.

Because sushi is a new experience for many people, I get to share my knowledge with my customers, and in doing so I am able to help them explore their tastes and introduce things to them. And if their experience in my restaurant is a good one, they want to learn more about sushi, about the food that is part of my Japanese heritage, and they may also include their family and friends in the experience.

I view this book as an extension of the hospitality and love I try always to share with my customers. My goal is to provide people who are curious about sushi with a base of knowledge that will help them explore and appreciate this cuisine to the fullest. As you read this guide to the many varieties and incarnations of sushi, I hope you find a great deal of useful information that will make you excited to visit your local *sushi-ya* and explore the many flavors of sushi.

The Origins of Sushi

In its beginning stages, sushi was nothing like the sushi we know now. The history of sushi dates back more than two thousand years, originally developed from a method of preserving fish that was introduced to the Japanese by the Chinese. In this preservation method, the *sakana* (fish) was salted and then placed on top of a layer of cooked rice in a container. Another layer of rice was spread on top of the fish, another layer of fish added on top of that, and so on until the container was full. Then a lid would be placed on top of the container, and a large stone would be set atop the lid to hold it down. The combination of salt and fermenting rice, which produced lactic acid, drew the moisture out of the fish and prevented it from spoiling.

With time, this preparation method—the forebear of sushi—spread through all of Japan. Different areas had their own styles of fermenting fish, of using salt and rice in different time increments to produce various tastes and textures. Some places fermented their fish for more than a year before they enjoyed it at the dinner table.

Japan is split between two regions, Kanto (east) and Kansai (west). The Kansai region was for many centuries the political and cultural center of Japan. The Kansai style of sushi (from the cities of Kyoto and Osaka) began the trend of serving rice with pickled fish as a topping. *Saba-zushi* or *bo-zushi* is said to have originated in Kyoto more than one thousand years ago. In this preparation rice is compacted with pickled mackerel on top and wrapped in bamboo leaves. Also from the Kansai style came *bara-zushi,* in which rice, fish, and many other ingredients are mixed together in a bowl; *oshi-zushi* (pressed sushi), also called *hako-zushi* (boxed sushi), in which a rectangular mold is used to compact rice and fish together; and *maki-mono,* which are the rolls that are one of the most popular and identifiable forms of sushi today.

When the capital of Japan shifted from Kyoto to Tokyo during the Edo period (1603-1876), the Kansai style of sushi gave way to Kanto-style sushi, or Edomae sushi, as it is often referred to now. Edo means Tokyo, and *Edomae* means "in front of Tokyo," referring to the waters of Tokyo Bay. In those days Tokyo Bay was rich in seafood, and fishermen gathered beautiful fish out of the sea and sold them to sushi chefs who then prepared the fish for Tokyo's citizens.

The *Edomae* style was the first to use a variety of fresh fish served on top of rice, which eventually developed into the hand-formed sushi, or *nigiri* sushi, that is commonly seen in today's *sushi-ya.*

Konnichi Wa: Welcome to the Sushi Experience
The Basic Ingredients and Preparations

....

The following brief introduction to the ingredients and preparations essential to sushi will acclimate you to the world of sushi and provide a foundation for learning more about sushi in the pages to come.

INGREDIENTS

SHARI (SUSHI RICE)
Japanese sushi rice is the main building block of sushi. *Kome* (uncooked white rice) is cooked and then mixed with the sushi chef's own recipe of vinegar, sugar, and salt.

SU (RICE VINEGAR)
Rice vinegar, sugar, and salt are added to *gohan* (cooked rice) to flavor it and to preserve it.

NORI (DRIED SEAWEED)
Half sheets or whole sheets of dried seaweed are used in creating *maki-mono* (rolled sushi), and will sometimes be used for *nigiri-zushi* (hand-formed sushi)—as a small belt to hold the topping onto the rice—or as a garnish in preparation of other sushi dishes.

Wasabi (Japanese Horseradish)

Japanese horseradish grows naturally in the flowing, fresh water of Japan's rivers. It has a nice, sweet and spicy flavor when it's freshly grated, but fresh wasabi is very difficult to find outside of Japan. Most wasabi comes to restaurants as powder, and water is mixed into it to create the paste that is used for sushi.

Shōyu (Soy Sauce)

Soy sauce is an essential part of the sushi experience. It is brewed from a mixture of fermented soybeans, salt, and wheat. Some *sushi-ya* in Japan create their own soy sauce, sometimes cooking it with sake (rice wine) to produce tamari (sushi soy). But there is a wide variety of premade soy sauce available, so most restaurants purchase theirs instead of brewing it themselves.

Gari (pickled ginger)

The Japanese are fond of pickled vegetables, and pickled ginger is one of the most popular due to its role in sushi. While *gari* is said to aid digestion, its main purpose in sushi is to cleanse the palate and prepare the mouth to enjoy a new flavor.

Refer to pages 16-17 for a photo of these ingredients.

KOME (SHORT-GRAINED RICE)

SHARI (SUSHI RICE)

16

GARI (PICKLED GINGER)

WASABI (JAPANESE HORSERADISH)

SU (RICE VINEGAR)

SHŌYU SASHI
(SOY SAUCE CONTAINER)

NORI (DRIED SEAWEED)

SHŌYU (SOY SAUCE)

The Essential Preparations

....

Although there are many ways to prepare sushi, these are the three most commonly seen presentations.

MAKI-MONO (ROLLED SUSHI)

Rolled sushi uses *shari,* nori, and wasabi as a framework for presenting the ingredients that give each roll its identity. *Hoso-maki* (thin roll) is the most basic form of *maki-mono*, with one or two ingredients in the middle surrounded by rice and wrapped in a half-sheet of seaweed with a hint of wasabi. *Futo-maki* (large roll) uses many ingredients, and *ura-maki* (inside-out roll) is presented with the rice on the outside. *Maki-mono* is made with a great variety of traditional and local ingredients, and sushi chefs all over the world enjoy being creative and developing their own signature rolls and styles.

NIGIRI-ZUSHI (HAND-FORMED SUSHI)

Although *nigiri-zushi* looks very simple—a topping on a ball of rice—the technique requires a great deal of practice to perfect. To create it, sushi chefs use both hands, and in one fluid motion they form the rice, then add a bit of wasabi to the underside of the fish and place it on top of the rice.

Sashimi (Sliced Raw Fish or Other Seafood)

This ancient style of serving carefully sliced raw fish is popular in Japan as a light appetizer, although you will find that many restaurants offer sashimi as a full meal. Sashimi allows one to enjoy and appreciate the flavor of the fish on its own, and can be an excellent sushi option for people on low-carbohydrate diets.

The Main Ingredient: Fresh Seafood

Sushi, in all its forms, has always been about enjoying fish and other food from the sea. In the following sections, you will learn about the many different types of seafood that are used to create delicious and healthy sushi.

Samurai Sushi
How to Use This Guide

....

Information about each item featured in this book is
separated into the following easy-to-understand categories:

≈ **ORIGIN:** Pertinent background information on each
item, such as specific portions of fish used for sushi or
ingredients for *maki-mono* (rolls) unique to Japanese
cuisine, is covered in this section. Special preparations
used for an item are also covered here.

▽ **INGREDIENTS:** Listed in this section of many of the entries
are the various ingredients used to create the specific item.

👁 **DISTINGUISHING CHARACTERISTICS:** This section, along
with the photo, makes it easy to identify different pieces
of nigiri, sushi, sashimi, and rolls.

🗋 **PRESENTATION:** Items in this book are served as sashimi or
nigiri-zushi unless otherwise specified in this section of
the entry. Certain items, such as *kani* (crab) or *maki-mono*,
are presented uniquely or served a number of different
ways. The text under this heading covers how these items
are generally served.

✕ **TASTE & TEXTURE:** The flavors and textures that characterize
each item are outlined in this section, making it easy to
find items that match your taste.

➤ **AVAILABILITY:** Not all the items covered in this book are available at every sushi restaurant (conversely, not every item available at every sushi restaurant is covered in this book). Information about where, when, and how frequently you can expect to find an item is covered in this section.

⌂ **PRICE:** Prices are relative to the overall cost of specific restaurants. This simple pricing scale helps identify the likely relative price of each item:
$—inexpensive
$$—moderately priced
$$$—expensive
$$$$—very expensive

! **ADDITIONAL INFO:** Interesting facts relating to each item are presented in this section of each entry.

来 **KANJI:** The name of each item is displayed in Japanese calligraphy (kanji) in the top right corner of each photo page.

Captions on the photo pages point out colors and patterns to look for in each item, as well as its ingredients.

The Japanese name for each item appears at the top of the page (and its English translation is listed in parentheses).

Types of Maguro (Tuna)
Identifying the Different Cuts of Sushi's Most Popular Fish

....

Today, tuna is the most popular and most enjoyed sushi item in the world. There are many different kinds of tuna used for sushi:

Mebachi Maguro (Bigeye Tuna)
Hon Maguro, Kuro Maguro (Bluefin Tuna)
Minami Maguro (Southern Tuna)
Kihada Maguro (Yellowfin Tuna)
Bincho, Binnaga (Albacore Tuna)
Kajiki Maguro (Swordfish)

Some of these names will change depending on where the fish come from. For example, *hon maguro* might be called *kuro* if it is from the waters of the Pacific Ocean, and *minami maguro* if it is from the Atlantic. Throughout the years I was training in Japan, I was told that a *sushi-ya* without tuna is not a *sushi-ya*. Tuna is that important to sushi. Ask the chef what kind of tuna they use and where it comes from.

鮪

Otoro (Very Fatty Tuna Meat)

ORIGIN: This is the richest part of the tuna. The *otoro* can only be cut from bigger fish (more than two hundred pounds), like *mebachi, kuro, hon,* and *minami maguro. Otoro* is taken from the section of the fish just below the head and gills, which is richest in oils and fats.

DISTINGUISHING CHARACTERISTICS: *Otoro* is bright pink and shiny in color. The patterns of fat within the meat are white and different from cut to cut. The fat may be in diagonal lines or appear in patterns like snowflakes in the meat. Lean tuna meat is normally red, so the fats and oils give it its pink color.

TASTE & TEXTURE: The sweetness that comes from the flavor of *otoro* and the mixture of the sushi rice together is absolutely delicious. And served on its own as sashimi, it is just as good, as the meat alone gives nice sweet and smoky flavors. At the beginning *otoro* is meaty, and as you bite into it and release the oils, it appears to melt in your mouth.

AVAILABILITY: *Otoro* is a rare find, because tuna with this type of meat are rare. Look for it in the wintertime when colder waters will result in more fat and oils in the fish.

PRICE: $$$$

ADDITIONAL INFO: Usually only true sushi connoisseurs know to ask for *otoro. Shimofuri,* or "falling frost," is the name often used to describe the marbled fat in *otoro.*

FAT CREATES
WHITE MARBLING

SHINY FROM OILS

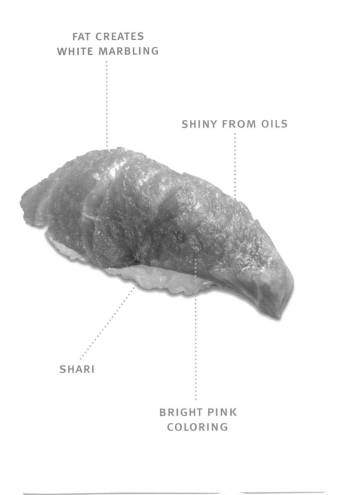

SHARI

BRIGHT PINK
COLORING

大トロ

*Chefs will often add extra wasabi
to otoro nigiri because the fish's
oils and fats counteract the spice.*

Toro *(Fatty Tuna Meat)*

≈ **ORIGIN:** Like *otoro,* the *toro* piece is cut from bigger tunas, like *kuro, hon,* or *minami maguro. Toro* is slightly less rich, but also has a good deal of fat and oils. It is cut from the belly area of a tuna just below the *otoro.* But if the fat content of a fish is low and no *otoro* exists, the *toro* cut will start just below the head and gills.

👁 **DISTINGUISHING CHARACTERISTICS:** *Toro* is a darker pink than *otoro* because it has slightly less fat. Like *otoro,* the fat can appear both in lines and marbled throughout the meat.

✕ **TASTE & TEXTURE:** *Toro* has a nice, sweet taste when combined with the sushi rice, and also tastes sweet on its own as sashimi. *Toro* has a stronger tuna flavor than *otoro* and is a bit more solid because of slightly less fat and oil content, but it still melts in your mouth as you're chewing and releases the oils.

⤳ **AVAILABILITY:** *Toro* is generally available, because tuna with the fat content needed to produce it are found frequently. Still, there may be times when it is scarce.

🛆 **PRICE:** $$$$

! **ADDITIONAL INFO:** In Japan *toro* plays a major part in sushi—almost everyone loves it. *Toro* is becoming popular in the rest of the world too.

トロ

FAT APPEARS IN
LINES AND MARBLED
THROUGHOUT THE MEAT

SHARI

DARKER PINK COLOR
THAN OTORO

Sushi restaurants usually only have toro or otoro. Seldomly are both available at once.

Bincho *(Albacore Tuna)*

≋ **ORIGIN:** At between five and ten pounds, *bincho* are much smaller than the other types of *maguro* used for sushi. Whereas larger tuna, such as *hon* or *mebachi maguro* are often caught individually due to their large size, *bincho* are netted in large numbers off the coast of areas such as Alaska.

👁 **DISTINGUISHING CHARACTERISTICS:** *Bincho* has a light pink or beige color. The outside of a piece of albacore sushi is often white because the chef has lightly seared the meat.

✂ **TASTE & TEXTURE:** In sharp contrast to the thickness of red meat tuna, *bincho* meat is very soft. The tuna flavor is also less strong than that of other *maguro*. A chef might sear the outside of this to add a smoky flavor, as well as to give more texture to the meat.

⤜ **AVAILABILITY:** *Bincho* will be available at most sushi restaurants.

♙ **PRICE:** $$

! **ADDITIONAL INFO:** Even though the color of *bincho* is so different from the larger red meat tunas, all tuna turns white when it is cooked. Also, you may have noticed that a lot of the canned tuna available in supermarkets is albacore.

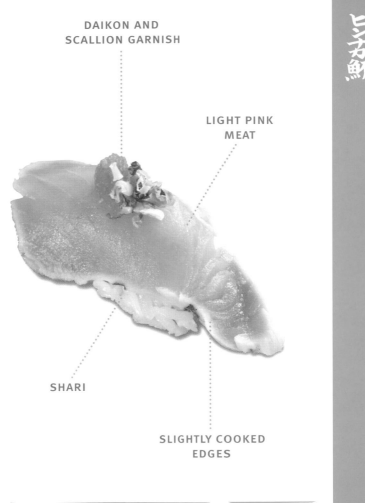

DAIKON AND
SCALLION GARNISH

ビンガ鮪

LIGHT PINK
MEAT

SHARI

SLIGHTLY COOKED
EDGES

Ask for ponzu *sauce on the side of your* bincho. *It compliments the* daikon *and scallion garnish.*

Chu-Toro (*Medium Toro, Half Toro*)

≈ ORIGIN: This cut of fish comes from the area between the lean meat on the sides of the tuna and the *toro* section. *Chu-toro* is usually found in bigger tunas, but sometimes when a smaller fish such as *kihada maguro* gets big it may have *chu-toro* meat. *Chu-toro* can also come from the sides of the fish or even sometimes the back of the fish near the skin if the fat content is high enough.

👁 DISTINGUISHING CHARACTERISTICS: The color of *chu-toro* depends on the type of fish and the cut. It may appear to have color gradations from red to pink, or it may have a lighter red color throughout.

✂ TASTE & TEXTURE: *Chu-toro* combines the delicate sweetness of lean tuna and a rich *toro* aftertaste. It also features the solid, meaty texture of lean tuna and the melt-in-your-mouth sensation of *toro*.

🐟 AVAILABILITY: This is available at most sushi restaurants.

🛍 PRICE: $$$

! ADDITIONAL INFO: The most popular and most widely used cut of tuna with oil and fat is *chu-toro,* mainly because of its availability. Some people prefer *chu-toro* because it's not as rich as *toro,* but most settle for *chu-toro* when the richer pieces are not available.

中トロ

COLOR GRADATION FROM
PINK TO RED

SHARI

*Only high-end sushi restaurants
will have all three types of* toro *at
the same time.*

Akami Maguro (Red Meat Tuna)

≋ | **ORIGIN:** All the meat on a lean tuna is used for *akami*, but generally true *akami* is cut from the back and sides of the tuna where there is little or no fat or oil content in the meat. The types of tuna used for *akami* change throughout the year. Sometimes the tuna come from the Pacific Ocean and other times from the Atlantic. *Kihada maguro* is generally the fish that *sushi-ya* will use for *akami*. This is the tuna called "ahi" in Hawaii. But don't ask for ahi, because you might get *aji* (horse mackerel).

👁 | **DISTINGUISHING CHARACTERISTICS:** Fresh *akami* is generally bright red, although it may also be a lighter red depending on what kind of tuna is used. *Mebachi akami* is ruby red, for example, and *kihada akami* is a duller red.

✂ | **TASTE & TEXTURE:** *Akami* has a bold flavor like that found in canned tuna, but of course it tastes much more fresh, and much lighter because it has no fat or oils. The texture is firm and meaty, almost like that of a steak.

👁 | **AVAILABILITY:** Red meat tuna is the most popular item in the sushi world. You will find it year-round at any sushi restaurant.

△ | **PRICE:** $$

! | **ADDITIONAL INFO:** Sometimes you will find *kajiki maguro* (swordfish) used as *akami*. This would be a treat to get a chance to try. *Kajiki* is not available often, but when it is, it's really good.

赤身

RUBY RED MEAT

SHARI

Akami *is a good introduction to raw fish because its texture resembles red meat.*

Types of *Shiromi* (*White Meat Fish*) The Healthiest Group of Fish Used for Sushi—Including Yellowtail, Bass, and Snapper

There are many fish in the *shiromi* group that are used for sushi. *Shiromi* are known for being low in fat and light-tasting—like *madai, hirame,* and *suzuki,* which are excellent as sushi and good for sashimi as well. The yellowtail family is in the white meat group also, even though they are richer in oils.

Usuzukuri (thinly sliced) is a wonderful way of enjoying *shiromi.* Cut almost paper-thin and served on a plate with chopped scallion and grated hot radish, this dish is served with a Japanese vinaigrette sauce called *ponzu.*

In the early days of *Edomae* sushi, *shiromi* were caught in many different parts of Japan. Now fish used for *shiromi* come from all parts of the world, and many are available year-round.

白身

Hamachi, Buri, Inada *(Yellowtail)*

ORIGIN: Although yellowtail is commonly referred to as *hamachi,* the name will often change with the maturity of the fish. *Buri* weigh more than ten pounds, *hamachi* are generally eight to ten pounds, and *inada* are less than eight pounds. *Hamachi* are caught all over, but Japanese *hamachi* is generally considered the best.

DISTINGUISHING CHARACTERISTICS: The meat from the belly, where the fish is rich in oil and fat, is white, and the leaner meat on the back part of the fish is tan to light pink.

TASTE & TEXTURE: Yellowtail is meaty, light, and sweet. The richest part, the belly part, of the *buri* (the mature yellowtail) is called *buri-toro* because, like *toro,* it melts in one's mouth.

AVAILABILITY: Yellowtail is best in the wintertime, when it is rich in fat. Because it is very popular throughout the world, most every *sushi-ya* will have it year-round.

PRICE: $$

ADDITIONAL INFO: This fish is in a group called *shusei-uo,* believed to bring good luck and success. Because hamachi is enjoyed at different stages of its life cycle, it is said that eating it will help you live a long life. *Buri* teriyaki is very popular in Japan. The collar part (*hamachi-no-kama*) is a delicacy, too. Some places might have this grilled with salt. If you get a chance, try it—you'll like it.

鮓

LIGHTER MEAT INDICATES
MORE OIL AND FAT

LEAN MEAT IS
DARKER PINK

SHARI

Negi hama-maki *(see page 150)*
is the most popular way to have
hamachi.

Kanpachi *(Amberjack)*

ORIGIN: *Kanpachi* is a type of yellowtail, grouped with the family because it shares the characteristic yellow tallow line that runs from head to tail. These fish are caught offshore in open water and weigh up to forty pounds.

DISTINGUISHING CHARACTERISTICS: *Kanpachi* sushi looks like *hamachi,* but the meat has a deeper tan color, similar to human skin, and might even appear golden in color.

TASTE & TEXTURE: *Kanpachi* has a buttery flavor and texture that distinguish it from other yellowtail.

AVAILABILITY: *Kanpachi* is best in the summer. A very popular fish in Japan, it is not well known to the rest of the sushi world. It is starting to be more available in North America, so you may see more of it.

PRICE: $$$

ADDITIONAL INFO: The buttery flavor and texture that make this fish desired are most evident in young *kanpachi*.

PINK COLOR INDICATES
LEANER MEAT

TAN OR "SKIN" COLOR

CAN APPEAR GOLDEN

SILVER COLORING ON MEAT
CLOSE TO THE SKIN

SHARI

Cuts of **kanpachi** *from near the skin are richer in oils and have more flavor.*

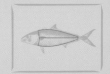

Shima Aji *(Yellow Jack)*

ORIGIN: This fish from the yellowtail family is shorter and stockier than *hamachi*. There are *zengo* (the heavy scales near the tail portion of the fish) on both sides of the fish, and a yellow line that runs across both sides and *zengo*. It is probably from these heavy scales, which are also found on *aji* (horse mackerel), that this fish got its name.

DISTINGUISHING CHARACTERISTICS: The meat of *shima aji* is white to golden in color. Like its fellow yellowtail, *kanpachi,* the meat is a deeper tan color than that of *hamachi* and other members of the yellowtail family.

TASTE & TEXTURE: Like most white fish, *shima aji* is light and not too fishy in flavor, with a slight sweetness. The texture is meaty and a little chewier than yellowtail.

AVAILABILITY: This fish, best to eat in the summer, is often not available—even in Japan. There seem to be more *shima aji* coming in from Hawaii now, so perhaps you'll have a chance to try it.

PRICE: $$$

ADDITIONAL INFO: *Shima aji* is considered a top-of-the-line sushi item in Japan.

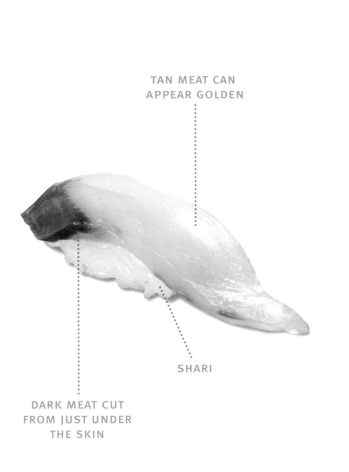

縞鯵

TAN MEAT CAN
APPEAR GOLDEN

SHARI

DARK MEAT CUT
FROM JUST UNDER
THE SKIN

This is regarded as the best fish within the yellowtail family, because it is most flavorful.

Madai (Red Sea Bream, Red Snapper)

≈ **ORIGIN:** *Madai,* a type of *tai* (sea bream, also called snapper), often come from New Zealand. They live in rocky coastal waters and swim through strong currents, which keeps them lean and meaty. The best fish are around fifteen to twenty pounds, but usually these are caught at six to ten pounds. Strong and bold-looking, the red color of the fish brings out the beauty it has to show.

👁 **DISTINGUISHING CHARACTERISTICS:** *Madai* meat is white and has red stripes on the side of the filet closest to the skin.

✂ **TASTE & TEXTURE:** The taste is light, with a subtle and elegant sweetness to it that you will not find in all white meat fish. As with most white meat fish, the fat content is low, and because of this, the texture is thicker and meatier.

👁 **AVAILABILITY:** *Madai* is best in the winter to spring months. In the *shiromi* group, *madai* is one of the most popular fish used for sushi in Japan.

🛍 **PRICE:** $$

❗ **ADDITIONAL INFO:** Also known as "the king of fish," *madai* has a signature role within Japanese culture. *Madai* are presented or shown in many celebrations and events, and even in festivals and religious rituals. For example, at the end of a sumo wrestling tournament, the winner will often hold up a whole, fresh *madai* as a symbol of victory.

RED STRIPING ON MEAT
CLOSE TO THE SKIN

WHITE MEAT

SHARI

Baby madai, *called* kodai *or* kasugo, *are pickled and served whole as sushi.*

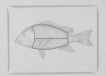

Hirame *(Sole or Flounder)*

≋ **ORIGIN:** *Hirame* is a flatfish, with eyes on the top left side of its body. The underside is white, and the top is grayish brown with black dots. *Hirame* are generally three to four pounds.

👁 **DISTINGUISHING CHARACTERISTICS:** *Hirame* is a pale white color, sometimes almost translucent in appearance.

✂ **TASTE & TEXTURE:** Because *hirame* is low in fat and high in protein, the taste is light and has a pleasant, clean aftertaste with very little fishiness. Although the meat seems very thick, it is not tough and is very easy to chew.

◔ **AVAILABILITY:** This fish is best enjoyed in the winter to spring months because its size is optimal during this period, and it has a bit of fat in it from the cold waters of winter. *Hirame* was once the favorite fish in Japan for *nigiri-zushi,* and it is gaining in popularity in the rest of the sushi world. But it can be difficult to find in a restaurant because it is often only available frozen, and chefs use only fresh *hirame* for sushi.

♤ **PRICE:** $$

! **ADDITIONAL INFO:** *Hirame* is very well regarded among Japanese women, because it is said that eating this fish benefits and beautifies one's skin.

鮃

PALE WHITE OR
TRANSLUCENT COLORING

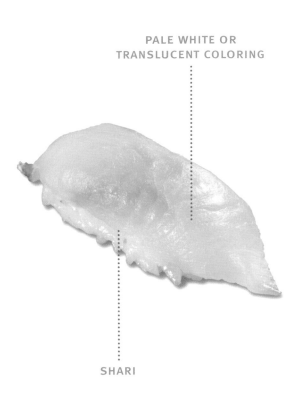

SHARI

Hirame *is unique because it yields
four filets, whereas most other fish
only have two.*

Suzuki *(Sea Bass)*

≋ **ORIGIN:** *Suzuki* is plentiful in the coastal waters of Japan, and many types of sea bass are fished all over the world. Like *hamachi*, the name of this fish changes as it grows, but only *suzuki* is used for sushi. It's called *koppa* at its youngest; *seigo* when it is six to ten inches; *fukko* at ten to fifteen inches; and then *suzuki* at the final stage of its growth of up to three feet.

👁 **DISTINGUISHING CHARACTERISTICS:** The meat is grayish-white with patterns of gray lines throughout.

✂ **TASTE & TEXTURE:** The flavor is on the light side, very subtle with a sweet aftertaste. It can taste like *kanpachi*, *shima aji*, or *hiramasa,* because like them it is a summer fish and is therefore less rich in fats and oils. *Suzuki* is very tender—easy to bite into and chew.

🜄 **AVAILABILITY:** This fish is best enjoyed in the summer months, when it is most mature. Within the last couple of years, *suzuki* has become more popular and is widely available, although there may be some places that do not offer it.

🜊 **PRICE:** $$

❗ **ADDITIONAL INFO:** *Suzuki* is in the *shusei-uo* category with *hamachi,* believed to bring good fortune and success because it is a fish eaten at different stages of its life cycle. It's rich in vitamin D and calcium, and is said to be good for bone development.

GRAYISH-WHITE MEAT

HINTS OF GRAY

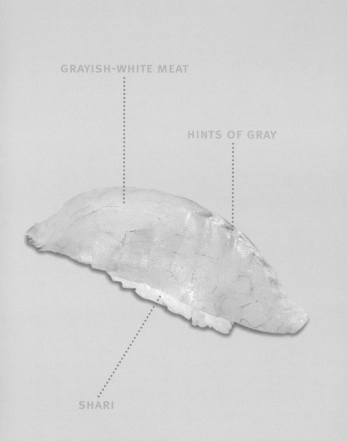

SHARI

Suzuki-no-arai is a dish made by shocking the meat in ice water and then serving it with ponzu sauce.

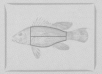

Karei (Halibut, Lemon Sole, a Type of Flounder)

≈ | **ORIGIN:** *Karei* is the general Japanese term for a flatfish whose eyes are on the right side of its head. Generally halibut or lemon sole are served as *karei*.

👁 | **DISTINGUISHING CHARACTERISTICS:** This fish is related to *hirame*, so the meat looks very similar—pale white or translucent.

✂ | **TASTE & TEXTURE:** The taste of *karei* is like *hirame,* a soft and delicate flavor that is light because Karei is low in fat. There is a gentle firmness to the meat.

⤳ | **AVAILABILITY:** Generally you will only see this fish a few times a year as sushi, because only the freshest *karei* are used, usually as a substitute for *hirame*.

♤ | **PRICE:** $$

! | **ADDITIONAL INFO:** *Karei,* a common fish in Japan, is enjoyed in many different ways. You might see it served grilled with salt or deep-fried. There are approximately six hundred kinds of flatfish known to us these days. The way to tell *hirame* and *karei* apart is easy: *hirame* has its eyes on the left, *karei* on the right. In Japan, *hidari* means "left," so it's easy to remember which side *hirame's* eyes are on.

PALE WHITE OR
TRANSLUCENT COLORING

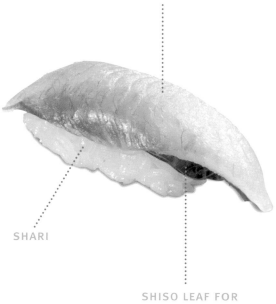

SHARI

SHISO LEAF FOR
DECORATION AND COLOR

*Karei and other light-tasting
fish are often served with shiso to
enhance the flavor.*

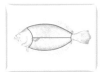

Hiramasa (*Amberjack, Kingfish*)

ORIGIN: *Hiramasa* is a yellowtail relative fished exclusively in the waters of Japan. Its characteristics are very close to those of *kanpachi,* with thicker tallow lines on both sides of the fish that run from head to tail.

DISTINGUISHING CHARACTERISTICS: To the untrained eye, *hiramasa* meat is nearly impossible to distinguish from *hamachi.* It can even be hard for experts to tell the difference between the two based simply on the appearance of the meat. Most chefs are only able to tell the difference between them by looking at the exterior of the whole fish.

TASTE & TEXTURE: Only experts will be able to tell the difference in taste between *hiramasa* and *hamachi*—they are both light and sweet-tasting. The meaty texture of *hiramasa* is nearly identical to that of *hamachi.*

AVAILABILITY: *Hiramasa* is only available in the summer months. It is a top-of-the-line sushi item in Japan, but it is not well-known in the rest of the world, so it will be difficult to find. Keep an eye out for it, and try it if you see it.

PRICE: $$$

ADDITIONAL INFO: This is one of the fish in the yellowtail family that is considered a delicacy. There are other fish, such as *kanpachi* and *shima aji,* within the same category that have similar tastes and textures, and are well regarded because they are only seasonally available.

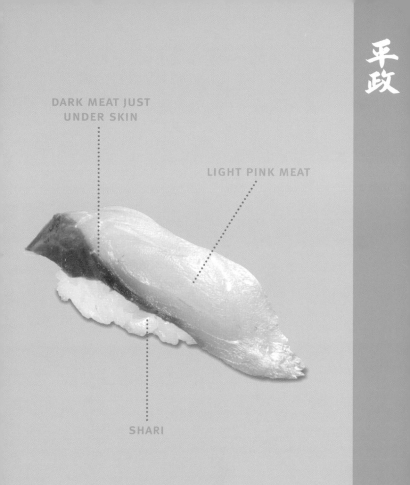

平政

DARK MEAT JUST
UNDER SKIN

LIGHT PINK MEAT

SHARI

During the season when it is
available, hiramasa *will often be*
served as hamachi.

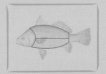

Types of Hikari-Mono (Shiny Fish) Small Fish That Are Pickled for Sushi

Hikari-mono are smaller fish with silvery skin that shines in the water. In sushi, these fish are pickled and preserved so that they can be enjoyed even beyond the normal availability of the fish.

Most *hikari-mono* go through a pickling process that has been used for many years. As we know, some of the first sushi was pickled. To prepare *hikari-mono*, the chef adds salt to a fresh filet. The amount of salt used and the length of time it is left on the fillet depends on the type of fish and its fat content. After a certain length of time, the salt is washed off, and the fish is marinated in vinegar. The acids in the vinegar cook the meat.

The quality of the *hikari-mono* is a good indicator of a chef's skill. It takes a lot of talent to perfect the balance between the salt and vinegar.

光り物

Shime Saba *(Pickled Mackerel)*

≈ **ORIGIN:** *Shime saba* are generally around two pounds. There are many different types of mackerel caught all over the world. We get ours from Norway.

👁 **DISTINGUISHING CHARACTERISTICS:** The *uchikawa* is silvery blue with darker lines through it. The meat is usually white, but *saba* may have some dark meat in the middle.

✕ **TASTE & TEXTURE:** *Shime saba* is very fishy. Although it is not as salty, the strength of its flavor is similar to anchovies. It has a nice, gentle, meaty feeling, and due to the level of oils and fat, it will give the effect of melting a bit in one's mouth.

🍶 **AVAILABILITY:** Fall to winter is usually the best time to eat *saba*. As they mature and the waters become colder, they start to get fat. *Saba* is available at most any *sushi-ya*.

♙ **PRICE:** $

! **ADDITIONAL INFO:** *Saba* has histidine, an amino acid, and is rich in omega oils, which is said to help your mind as you get older, protecting against Alzheimer's and other diseases afflicting the aged.

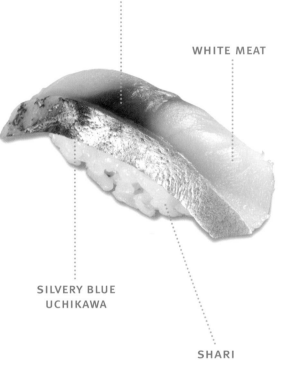

DARK MEAT INDICATES
THIS PIECE WAS CUT FROM
THE MACKEREL'S MIDDLE

WHITE MEAT

SILVERY BLUE
UCHIKAWA

SHARI

Most hikari-mono *are served with
the* uchikawa *(the skin beneath the
skin) showing.*

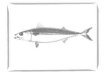

Kohada *(Gizzard Shad)*

≈ | **ORIGIN:** This small, spineless, silvery fish is part of the herring family. *Kohada* is another fish whose name changes as it matures. It will be called *konoshiro* or *shinko* at a young age, *kohada* at a slightly older age, and *nakatsumi* at a mature age. *Kohada* is a very small fish, usually not much more than a few inches long.

👁 | **DISTINGUISHING CHARACTERISTICS:** *Kohada* meat is white with a pinkish hint. The silver coloring and black spots of the under skin make it appear that the meat has not been skinned. But don't worry—the outer skin has been removed.

✄ | **TASTE & TEXTURE:** With its strong fishy flavor, *Kohada* tastes very similar to *shime saba*. It is marinated in vinegar for a long period of time to soften the tiny bones in the meat. *Kohada* has a nice, meaty texture and is not very rich in oils.

◐ | **AVAILABILITY:** *Kohada* is only available as sushi in the winter, when this fish is at the right age. *Kohada* has been around a long time in Japan, and it's starting to appear outside of Japan more often.

△ | **PRICE:** $

! | **ADDITIONAL INFO:** In Japan, when you ask for *hikari-mono* they will usually give you *kohada*.

小鰭

WHITE MEAT
WITH A PINKISH HINT
NEAR THE SKIN

GINGER AND SCALLION
CHANGE THE FLAVOR

SHARI

SILVER COLORING AND BLACK
SPOTS MAKE THE SKIN
APPEAR INTACT

*Ginger and scallion are added
to mellow the very fishy flavor
of kohada.*

Aji *(Horse Mackerel)*

≈ **ORIGIN:** The most popular types of *aji* are *ma-aji, ki-aji,* and *kuro-aji*—the Japanese name changes depending on the waters where they are caught, but in English this is simply "horse mackerel." *Aji* are fished all over the world, but restaurants usually receive their *aji* from Japan, Hawaii, Australia, or New Zealand.

👁 **DISTINGUISHING CHARACTERISTICS:** The meat of *aji* is a light tan. The *uchikawa* has a shiny silver color.

✂ **TASTE & TEXTURE:** Like *saba,* *aji* has a fishy flavor, but it is much more mellow than *saba* because it is salted and marinated in vinegar for a shorter period of time. If you like tuna or yellowtail, you should try *aji*.

🐟 **AVAILABILITY:** *Aji* is a basic sushi item in Japan, but it is now becoming more available outside of Japan, and will probably continue to gain popularity.

💰 **PRICE:** $$

❗ **ADDITIONAL INFO:** A very popular dish in Japan using *aji* is called *aji-no tataki*. In this presentation the meat is chopped or cut into small pieces and arranged with ginger and scallion. Onion and miso can be added to enhance the flavor. An artful chef might use the *aji* skeleton as a serving dish.

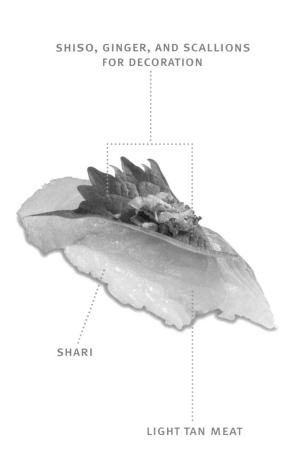

鯵

SHISO, GINGER, AND SCALLIONS
FOR DECORATION

SHARI

LIGHT TAN MEAT

Shiso, ginger *and* scallions *are
often added* to a piece of aji *purely
to enhance the appearance.*

Types of Ebi (*Shrimp, Prawns*)
Common Types of Shrimp and Prawns Used for Sushi

....

There are more than a thousand different types of shrimp and prawns in the waters of our planet. *Kuruma* (wheel) shrimp, the signature *ebi* of sushi, was the first to be used for *nigiri* in *Edomae* sushi. Black tiger prawns are the ones most used for sushi these days.

Usually *ebi* is served as a cooked item, but there are shrimp and prawns that are served raw, such as *ama-ebi, botan-ebi,* and *odori* (live *kuruma*). To prepare *ebi,* the head is removed and the tail is skewered on bamboo to prevent it from curling, then boiled, peeled, and butterflied.

Today, *ebi* is one of the most popular sushi items around the world, often the first thing a sushi beginner would try.

蝦

Ebi *(Black Tiger Shrimp)*

≋ **ORIGIN:** *Ebi* is the universal Japanese term for shrimp or prawns, but the most common type of prawn served as *ebi* all over the world is the black tiger shrimp, which gets its name from the dark color of its shell and the dark gray stripes on its back that resemble a tiger's stripes.

👁 **DISTINGUISHING CHARACTERISTICS:** Even though the shells of these shrimp are dark in color, *ebi* has white meat with red- or orange-colored stripes.

✂ **TASTE & TEXTURE:** The taste and texture of cooked shrimp are familiar to most people. Ebi have a light flavor with a sweet aftertaste, and are solid and meaty.

>⊃ **AVAILABILITY:** As one of the most popular sushi items, *ebi* will always be available.

△ **PRICE:** $$

! **ADDITIONAL INFO:** Black tiger is the most widely used sushi shrimp, but *kuruma ebi* (wheel shrimp) were the first shrimp to be served as sushi in Japan. They are not often found on menus outside of Japan, and one particular preparation of *kuruma ebi* is very rarely offered anywhere but in Japan. When *kuruma ebi* is served "alive," it is called *odori ebi* or "dancing shrimp," because the meat moves as if it is dancing. When you order *odori,* the chef first shows you the whole live shrimp, then tears off the head. The tail is then shelled, and the tail meat is butterflied and served *nigiri* style. The meat is still moving as you eat it.

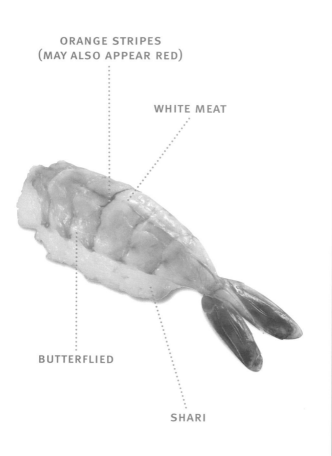

ORANGE STRIPES
(MAY ALSO APPEAR RED)

WHITE MEAT

BUTTERFLIED

SHARI

蝦

When forming ebi nigiri *a chef tries to make the whole piece look like a large shrimp tail.*

Botan Ebi (*Spot Prawns*)
Ama Ebi (*Sweet Shrimp*)

ORIGIN: *Botan ebi* is the largest of the shrimps used for *ama ebi,* sometimes growing as big as a small lobster. Usually this is served one whole shrimp to one piece of sushi. Spot prawns used in North America come from the Pacific Northwest and Alaska. In Japan, spot prawns come from the Hokkaido area.

DISTINGUISHING CHARACTERISTICS: The raw meat is light gray to white, with a red outer layer.

TASTE & TEXTURE: *Botan ebi* is very sweet, like its *ama ebi* counterparts, and is meaty and a bit slimy.

AVAILABILITY: Spot prawns are very popular in Japan and can be found in most any *sushi-ya.* People in the rest of the world tend not to enjoy raw shrimp as much, so many places do not offer these on the menu. Again, it never hurts to ask the chef at your local restaurant.

PRICE: $$$

ADDITIONAL INFO: In Japan, *botan ebi* is considered to be a high-class or high-society type of sushi because it is larger in size than the other shrimp that are served as *ama ebi.*

**BUTTERFLIED
THROUGH THE BACK**

**RED-AND-PINK
OUTER LAYER**

WHITE MEAT

SHARI

**MORE INTRICATE
FAN TAIL**

牡丹蝦

*Another smaller shrimp served as
ama ebi is aka ebi, or red shrimp.*

Shakko (*Mantis Shrimp*)

≈ **ORIGIN:** Mantis shrimp is not really a shrimp, but is part of the largest class of crustaceans on the planet, the *Stomatopods*. This shrimp looks more like an insect than a shrimp—kind of scary. It is served cooked.

👁 **DISTINGUISHING CHARACTERISTICS:** *Shakko* has a purple to gray color, even when it's cooked.

✕ **TASTE & TEXTURE:** Even though *shakko* looks different, the taste is just like any shrimp. It's served with *nitsume* (eel sauce) over it. *Shakko* is a *nimono neta* (a cooked item), so the texture has a meatiness to it like shrimp and crab.

⟫ **AVAILABILITY:** In Japan, *shakko* is a well-known sushi item, but elsewhere it is new enough that most people are not yet familiar with it. *Shakko* from the waters of Tokyo Bay are very popular, and especially *shakko* that come from a fishing harbor in Tsurumi-ku of Yokohama. They are best in the summer months, before spawning, when they are rich with eggs.

⌂ **PRICE:** $$$

! **ADDITIONAL INFO:** *Shakko* means "garage" in Japan. *Sha* is "car," and *ko* means "place." When you're at a sushi bar ask for "garage" and you will get *shakko,* and you'll also get a laugh out of the chef.

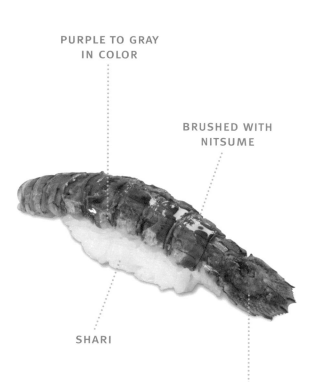

蝦蛄

PURPLE TO GRAY
IN COLOR

BRUSHED WITH
NITSUME

SHARI

DIFFERENT TAIL THAN
OTHER SHRIMP

People who like shakko *prefer*
komochi shakko, *which is mantis
shrimp fertile with eggs.*

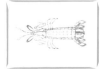

Types of Kai *(Shellfish)*
Shellfish Used for Sushi, Including Abalone, Scallops, and Razor Clams

....

There are two types of shellfish: the bivalves, which have a top and bottom shell; and the single-valve clams, which have only one shell, like a snail.

Around the waters of Japan, there are more than five hundred kinds of shellfish. The Japanese eat about half of the different kinds. For sushi, there are some thirty kinds of shellfish available in the markets. *Kai* were first used during the Edo period, but were served cooked because this allowed chefs to sell these for a longer period of time after the body was removed from the shell. Now that we have refrigerated food infrastructures, *kai* are available raw for sushi.

貝

Akagai (Red Clam, Ark Shell)

≈ | **ORIGIN:** The ark shell is considered the superior shellfish item for sushi. Its shell is ribbed and it is generally about three inches across, from its hinge to the opposite side of the shell. *Akagai* live in the brackish water near the mouths of rivers.

👁 | **DISTINGUISHING CHARACTERISTICS:** The meat is usually red and can appear orange as well. There are three parts to *akagai* used for sushi: the body, the threadlike filaments (*himo*) that connect the body to the shell, and the adductor muscle (*hashira*). The latter two are considered more desirable by connoisseurs. Chefs add cuts to the body to tenderize it and for show.

✂ | **TASTE & TEXTURE:** The taste of *akagai* is like the scent of the ocean with a sweet clam flavor. The body is meatier and chewier than the *himo* and *hashira,* which are crunchy.

⟩⚬ | **AVAILABILITY:** Winter to spring is the best time for this clam. *Akagai* is a very well known and popular clam in Japan, but it is rarely available at sushi restaurants elsewhere.

🏷 | **PRICE:** $$

! | **ADDITIONAL INFO:** The bright red color of *akagai* is due to the presence of hemoglobin in its bloodstream. This is rare, and contributes to the mystique of this highly regarded clam.

赤貝

SMALL CUTS ADDED TO
TENDERIZE AND ORNAMENT THE CLAM

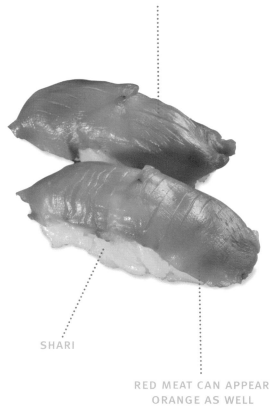

SHARI

RED MEAT CAN APPEAR
ORANGE AS WELL

*Chefs cut different patterns in the
meat to enhance the appearance of
many pieces of sushi.*

Awabi (Abalone)

≋ **ORIGIN:** *Awabi* has only a top shell. While it moves like a snail, it does not look like one—at a glance *awabi* resemble a rock or piece of coral. Most of the *awabi* that is eaten and used for sushi today comes from four major parts of the world. *Awabi* that come from the waters of Japan during the summer are said to be the best. *Awabi* also come from Australia, South Africa, and the west coast of North America.

👁 **DISTINGUISHING CHARACTERISTICS:** *Awabi* meat is tan with dark edges.

✂ **TASTE & TEXTURE:** *Awabi* has a very fresh ocean flavor that emerges with each bite. It is the chewiest clam used for sushi. The meat is very tough, especially the dark meat on the edges.

🐟 **AVAILABILITY:** *Awabi,* a protected species, are commercially cultured in Japan and elsewhere. Abalone is a popular sushi item in Japan and around Asia. The tough texture shows freshness, and this is what is liked there. Outside Japan, chewy items such as *tako* (octopus, see page 110) or *ika* (squid, see page 106) are less popular overall, simply because people's tastes are different.

🛆 **PRICE:** $$$$

❗ **ADDITIONAL INFO:** Adding to their mystique as a valuable shellfish, *awabi* have mother-of-pearl, used often in making watches and jewelry, lining their shells.

SMALL CUTS TENDERIZE AND
DECORATE THE MEAT

TAN MEAT

SHARI

DARKER EDGES

Mushi awabi, *or steamed
abalone, is a very popular sushi
item in Japan.*

Hokkigai (Surf Clam), *Ubagai*

~~ **ORIGIN:** This shell is on the brown side, hard and thick. These are larger clams, with thicker shells, that flourish in cold waters. Normally these clams are three to four inches across, but can grow as big as six inches or more.

👁 **DISTINGUISHING CHARACTERISTICS:** The meat is white to tan, with reddish-purple tips. The *himo* are also served as a sushi item.

✂ **TASTE & TEXTURE:** This clam has a very pleasant and mellow ocean flavor with a nice sweetness that emerges as you chew it. This would be a good clam to try as an introduction to *kai*. The meat of this clam can be tough. I like to put little cuts in the meat to tenderize it, which helps one to enjoy this clam a lot more.

⌛ **AVAILABILITY:** *Hokkigai* are best in the winter to spring months when they are larger, and are widely available and used as sushi all over the world.

👜 **PRICE:** $$

! **ADDITIONAL INFO:** *Ubagai* is the formal name for this clam in Japan, but it is known as *hokkigai* all over the world.

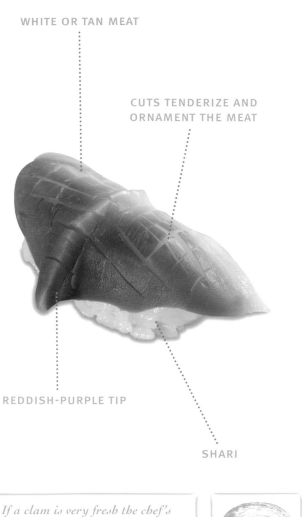

WHITE OR TAN MEAT

CUTS TENDERIZE AND
ORNAMENT THE MEAT

北
寄
貝

REDDISH-PURPLE TIP

SHARI

*If a clam is very fresh the chef's
cuts in the meat will expand and
open up.*

Hotategai *(Scallop)*

≈ **ORIGIN:** Scallops are bivalves, with a flat bottom shell and a larger, rounded top shell. Usually when you see scallops in a restaurant or market they are fairly small, but these can grow as big as your hand.

👁 **DISTINGUISHING CHARACTERISTICS:** The color is off-white to beige when it is served raw. When cooked in a sweet soy sauce, it will be light brown in color.

✂ **TASTE & TEXTURE:** Most people know that scallops taste sweet and light when cooked. Raw, they taste a bit fishier and even sweeter. Often these are served with *nitsume*. *Hotategai* is served raw more often now since it is available fresh. As you bite into the raw *hotategai* sushi, the meat is soft but firm. If you get it cooked, it's a bit more firm and meaty.

🐟 **AVAILABILITY:** This is a very common item both in Japan and in North America. You will find *hotategai* at most sushi restaurants.

♙ **PRICE:** $$

! **ADDITIONAL INFO:** *Hotategai* is thought of as a *nimono neta* (a cooked item) in the Tokyo area, because these are native to Hokkaido and Tohoku, and traditionally were not available fresh to sushi restaurants. But in the areas where these come from they have always been served raw.

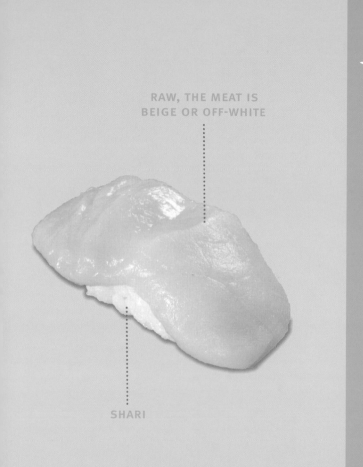

帆立貝

RAW, THE MEAT IS
BEIGE OR OFF-WHITE

SHARI

Like ebi, hotategai *are served
butterflied and spread out across
the ball of rice.*

Mirugai (Geoduck, Horse Neck Clam, Giant Clam)

ORIGIN: *Mirugai* are among the biggest clams used for sushi, sometimes growing to a couple of feet in length. There are two parts to *mirugai* used for sushi: the body and the neck, or "siphon." The neck sticks out from the shell and acts as a siphon, ingesting water and nutrients. A lot of geoduck comes from the Pacific Northwest, and much of it is exported to Japan. Hokkaido has its own *mirugai,* which are a bit shorter than those found in North America.

DISTINGUISHING CHARACTERISTICS: *Mirugai* is light brown to white in color.

TASTE & TEXTURE: The taste is like the ocean and is sweet. Chefs often put cuts in the meat of the clam to tenderize it, so that when you eat it, it's crunchy not chewy.

AVAILABILITY: *Mirugai* is best from February to June, but is available year-round in *sushi-ya* all over the world.

PRICE: $$$

ADDITIONAL INFO: In Japan, geoduck imported from the United States is called *shiroi mirugai,* or "white *mirugai.*" Some people say that *mirugai* is an aphrodisiac.

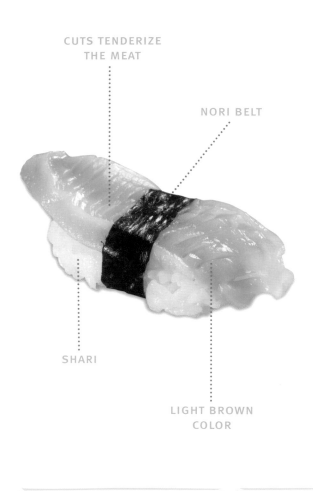

CUTS TENDERIZE
THE MEAT

NORI BELT

SHARI

LIGHT BROWN
COLOR

海
松
貝

Geoduck are usually alive until the chef cuts them. The fresher these are, the crunchier the meat.

Tairagai *(Razor Clam)*

≈ **ORIGIN:** The shape of the *tairagai* is different from that of other clams. It looks like a fan. Inside there is a big adductor muscle, which is the main part of this triangular-shaped clam, and only the muscle is served.

👁 **DISTINGUISHING CHARACTERISTICS:** The color is white to tan, and it looks exactly the same as a scallop.

✂ **TASTE & TEXTURE:** These have a pleasant oceanic flavor with a hint of sweetness. Although *tairagai* look like scallops, their texture is firmer.

🐟 **AVAILABILITY:** In Japan, *tairagai* are found in the waters that separate Hokkaido from the main island. Although they are caught in both fall and spring months, fall is the best time to enjoy this clam because it is meatier and sweeter. This is commonly served in Japan and is becoming more widely available elsewhere.

🛍 **PRICE:** $$

! **ADDITIONAL INFO:** *Tairagai* is nearly indistinguishable in appearance from *hotategai*. Unless the chef told you that you were eating *tairagai,* you might not notice the difference, although *tairagai* has a stronger flavor and slightly tougher meat than *hotategai.*

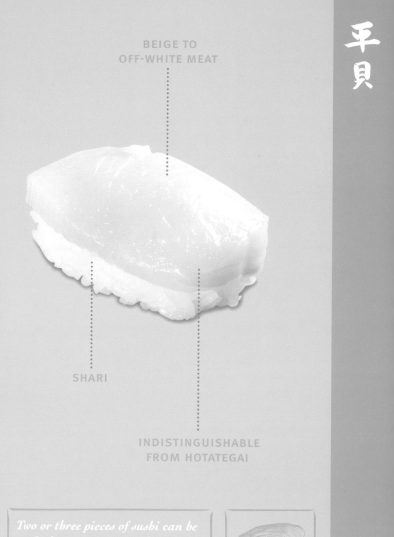

平
貝

BEIGE TO
OFF-WHITE MEAT

SHARI

INDISTINGUISHABLE
FROM HOTATEGAI

Two or three pieces of sushi can be made from one tairagai *because they are larger clams.*

Torigai (Cockle)

≋ **ORIGIN:** The *torigai* has one of the most beautiful shells of the clams used for sushi. They are generally about four inches across. The body of the clam is shaped like a foot. Although there are many different types of cockle found all over the world, it is mainly caught for sushi in the waters north of Kyushu, the large island located at the southwest end of the main island of Japan.

👁 **DISTINGUISHING CHARACTERISTICS:** The color of *torigai* can be black, brown, or white. When you order *torigai* you may notice that it appears to have a tail sticking up into the air. This is actually the "neck" of the clam.

✂ **TASTE & TEXTURE:** *Torigai* has a fresh ocean flavor and is sweet. It is not as chewy as many other clams.

⋈ **AVAILABILITY:** *Torigai* is available in the winter to spring months when they are harvested in Japan. It is generally only available frozen to restaurants outside Japan. We may start to see these brought in fresh to North America if they become a more popular item.

△ **PRICE:** $$

! **ADDITIONAL INFO:** Generally the meat of the *torigai* is very thin, so the thicker and meatier the particular cockle, the more value it has. *Torigai* is very stiff when it is fresh, so the chef will often form the *nigiri* with the neck of the clam sticking up to display its freshness.

COLOR CAN BE WHITE,
BROWN, OR EVEN BLACK

鳥貝

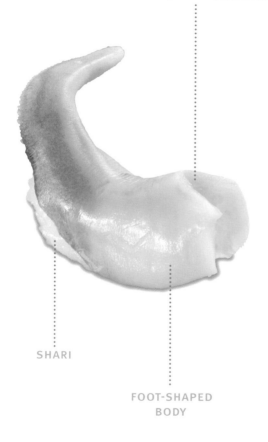

SHARI

FOOT-SHAPED
BODY

You can gauge the freshness of torigai by how straight the neck stands up.

Types of Kani (Crab)
Including King, Snow, Blue, and Dungeness Crab

There are many kinds of *kani* used in the world of sushi today, although it is a relatively new sushi item. In Japan, *kani* is an ingredient frequently used in hot pots (*nabe*), cooked with vegetables, or served as a *sunomono* (salad with a vinaigrette sauce).

At a *sushi-ya* you are likely to see crab served a number of ways: as an ingredient in California rolls, spider rolls, and even as *nigiri-zushi* or sashimi.

Each area of the world seems to have access to a different type of *kani,* and these regional supplies make using crab for sushi even more interesting. If you like crab, be open to eating what is native to the area where you're eating, because what you find might be really good and only available there.

蟹

Matsubagani, Zuwai Gani
(Snow Crab)

ORIGIN: This crab has long, skinny legs and looks like a spider. The name will differ across Japan, but it is the same crab and will always be called "snow crab" in North America. Around Japan, they are caught from the Japan Sea up to Hokkaido. In North America, snow crab come from Alaska and Russia's Bering Sea.

DISTINGUISHING CHARACTERISTICS: The meat is white with red coloring on the portions that were closest to the shell.

PRESENTATION: Snow crab is served as *nigiri,* sashimi, or as part of a roll.

TASTE & TEXTURE: The snow crab is sweet, fresh and delicious, and it has nice, firm meat.

AVAILABILITY: *Matsubagani* are best in the winter months when they are more mature. This is the most widely used type of crab in sushi. If a *sushi-ya* has crab, it will probably be snow crab. You should be able to order this at most any sushi restaurant.

PRICE: $$

ADDITIONAL INFO: In Japan, *matsubagani* are a very popular ingredient in *nabe,* where seafood, vegetables, and other items are mixed together as in a stew, and families or groups of friends share and eat from the same pot.

WHITE MEAT

PINKISH OR RED
COLORING ON OUTSIDE

ずわい蟹

NORI BELT

SHARI

Matsubagani *have skinny legs, so
it usually takes two or three legs to
make one piece of* nigiri-zushi.

Taraba Gani *(King Crab)*

≋ **ORIGIN:** *Taraba gani* is called the king of crabs because with legs spread they can reach a width of up to five feet. These are mostly harvested in northern areas such as Alaska, Russia, and Hokkaido. The top of the shell is bright red to orange and the bottom is white. Generally only the legs and claws are used for sushi.

👁 **DISTINGUISHING CHARACTERISTICS:** The meat is primarily white but will also have a red color like its shell, similar to that found on shrimp.

🍣 **PRESENTATION:** *Taraba gani* is one of the crabs used for *nigiri-zushi,* and it will usually be presented with a *nori* belt to hold it on the rice. It is very popular as sashimi as well. You can also ask the chef to serve this crab as part of a roll.

✂ **TASTE & TEXTURE:** King is among the most delicious crabs, with an incredible natural sweetness. The legs and claws have a very pleasant meaty texture.

🐟 **AVAILABILITY:** Although this is available all over Japan, it can be difficult to get anywhere but in North America on the west coast because it is expensive.

🛍 **PRICE:** $$$$

❗ **ADDITIONAL INFO:** Studies say that king crabs can live more than thirty years, and male crabs weighing more than twenty pounds have been caught.

王蟹

NORI BELT HOLDS
DELICATE MEAT TOGETHER

WHITE MEAT

SHARI

RED OUTER
COLORING

*King crab are so large that often
only a slice out of the thigh or claw
will make a piece of sushi.*

Soft-Shell Crab, Blue Crab

≈ **ORIGIN:** There is no Japanese name for blue or soft-shell crab, because it is native to the waters of the east coast of the United States.

👁 **DISTINGUISHING CHARACTERISTICS:** Soft-shell crab is always served coated and fried with a bit of flour or cornstarch, so it is both dark and golden brown.

🍥 **PRESENTATION:** Although some *sushi-ya* might serve a blue crab appetizer with a whole fried blue crab and *ponzu* sauce, this will most always be served as a part of the spider roll (see page 146).

✂ **TASTE & TEXTURE:** The sweetness you normally taste in crabmeat is very subtle in soft-shell crab. The texture is very crunchy.

⊃ **AVAILABILITY:** Soft-shell crab is a U. S. product, popular on the east coast. Most *sushi-ya* in the United States serve spider rolls, so you will be able to get this nearly everywhere. Since this crab is native to the U. S., it is considered a delicacy in Japan and can be hard to find outside of the U. S.

🜶 **PRICE:** $$$

! **ADDITIONAL INFO:** Once the blue crab sheds its shell, crabbers have only four hours to get it out of the water before the new shell begins to harden. The blue crab gets its name from the blue coloring on the legs and claws of the male.

青蟹

COATED AND FRIED BROWN
IN FLOUR AND CORNSTARCH

NORI BELT

SHARI

These smaller crabs are fried whole, and often half of the crab will be served as one piece of sushi.

Dungeness Crab

ORIGIN: This sushi item has no Japanese name because it is native to the waters of the Pacific Northwest. The body of this crab is fat, its legs proportionally shorter than other crabs, and its shell is a brownish red.

DISTINGUISHING CHARACTERISTICS: As a sushi item, Dungeness crab is served cooked, so the meat is white with some red coloring.

PRESENTATION: Dungeness crab is served as *nigiri*, sashimi, or as a roll. Some people may ask for a California roll (see page 138) with Dungeness crab, or this may be served as a simple Dungeness crab roll.

TASTE & TEXTURE: Dungeness crab has an appealing sweetness, and the crab flavor is very nice and strong. Like most other crab meat, it is meaty but light.

AVAILABILITY: You will probably find this served only on the Pacific Coast of the United States and Canada.

PRICE: $$$

ADDITIONAL INFO: This crab got its name from Old Town Dungeness on the Olympic Peninsula of Washington. Interestingly, Dungeness and all other crabs are cannibalistic, although they eat a wide variety of sealife.

RED COLORING

WHITE MEAT

NORI BELT

SHARI

The shoulder meat and certain parts of the body of these and other crabs are often used for rolls.

Additional Sushi Items
Other Favorites Such as Salmon and Eel

In the following pages are some other items that are being used as sushi today but do not fit into any particular category. Items such as *ika, tako,* and *anago* are long-time favorites, while *katsuo, sake,* and *ankimo* are relatively new to sushi.

他の魚

Katsuo (*Bonito*)

≈ **ORIGIN:** *Katsuo* is a red meat fish that is related to tuna and mackerel, and generally weighs between five and twenty pounds. In Japan, *katsuo* comes from the waters off an island called Shikoku, but much of the *katsuo* served in North America comes from Hawaii.

👁 **DISTINGUISHING CHARACTERISTICS:** The meat of the bonito is red. When serving this, chefs will leave the skin on, which is silvery or dark blue, and salt and grill it, turning it brown. This preparation is called *yaki-shimo*.

✂ **TASTE & TEXTURE:** Bonito tastes much like tuna. It can be rich in oil and fats like *toro,* or lean and meaty like *akami*. In the springtime, *katsuo* has less oil, so the taste is much like *akami* tuna. This fish gets richer in fats and oils in the fall months, and some say it is superior to tuna.

⋗ **AVAILABILITY:** *Katsuo* is said to be best in the spring and fall. They are a very popular item in Japan, native to the waters of the Pacific Ocean. Bonito is often available at sushi restaurants on the west coast of North America, but may be difficult to find on the east coast.

🍶 **PRICE:** $$

! **ADDITIONAL INFO:** *Katsuo-dashi,* a bonito-based soup, is eaten daily by many Japanese people. *Katsuo-no-tataki* is also a very popular dish in which cooked bonito is served with chopped scallion, grated ginger, chopped garlic, and *ponzu* sauce.

鰹

GINGER AND SCALLION
ACCENT THE FLAVOR

RED MEAT

GRILLED SKIN

SHARI

A fishy-tasting yellowtail relative, katsuo is often served with ginger and scallion to reduce the fishiness.

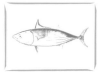

Anago (*Sea Eel, Conger Eel*)

≋ **ORIGIN:** *Anago* are long and skinny, like a snake, and can grow up to ten feet in length, although the younger and smaller *anago* are preferable for sushi. They like to bury themselves in the sands or hide in the rocks of Japanese coastal waters.

👁 **DISTINGUISHING CHARACTERISTICS:** *Anago* is served cooked with *nitsume* (eel sauce) brushed over it. The color of this sushi can be white or light brown, but is usually dark brown because of the sauce.

✕ **TASTE & TEXTURE:** The taste is not rich, but mellow and sweet. The texture is soft and delicate, almost melting in one's mouth.

⤳ **AVAILABILITY:** *Anago* is available at sushi restaurants all year, but is best during the summer. In the early days of sushi, *anago* caught in Tokyo Bay were used as a *nimono neta* (cooked item) for *Edomae* sushi. Now, they are cultured in different parts of Asia and come in from China and Korea.

⚖ **PRICE:** $$

❗ **ADDITIONAL INFO:** *Nitsume* is a very popular ingredient in Japanese cuisine, and many sushi chefs make their own. When a sushi chef receives a delivery of *anago*, he boils a number of them whole in a pot. To make *nitsume,* he then removes the *anago,* adds his recipe of soy sauce and sugar to the stock, and reduces the broth until it is thick and sticky.

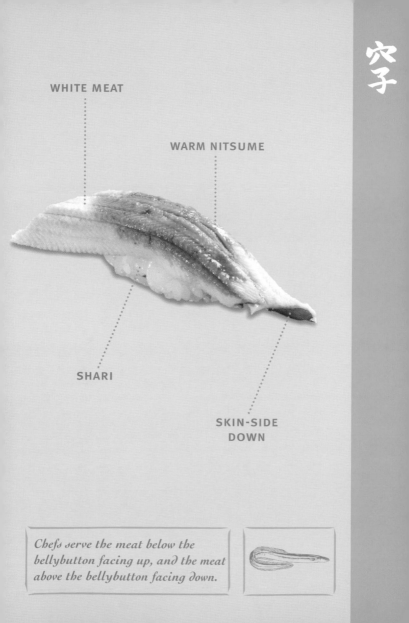

穴子

WHITE MEAT

WARM NITSUME

SHARI

SKIN-SIDE DOWN

Chefs serve the meat below the bellybutton facing up, and the meat above the bellybutton facing down.

Ankimo *(Monkfish Liver)*

ORIGIN: *Ankimo* is a very unique sushi item because the meat of the fish from which it is taken is not used for sushi. Once the liver is removed, monkfish are served steamed or boiled. In Japan, the meat of the fish is usually used for a *nabe* (hot pot).

DISTINGUISHING CHARACTERISTICS: Tan, orange, or gray in color, the shape of *ankimo* will differ with the size of the fish from which the liver is taken. It is generally served as a *gunkan-maki,* or "battleship sushi."

TASTE & TEXTURE: *Ankimo* has the flavor and creaminess of fish pâté.

AVAILABILITY: *Ankimo*, very popular in Japan, is widely available, but elsewhere it does not carry the same status and you are less likely to encounter it. Monkfish is readily available from fish suppliers, so if you don't see *ankimo* on the menu at your favorite *sushi-ya,* it doesn't hurt to ask the chef.

PRICE: $$$

ADDITIONAL INFO: Some people call monkfish meat the poor man's lobster, but its liver is a delicacy and it is sometimes used for foie gras. In Japan, *ankimo* is believed to give you stamina because it is so rich in oils.

鮟
肝

SHISO LEAF
FOR DECORATION

DAIKON AND SCALLION
ACCENT THE FLAVOR

TAN
COLORING

ORANGE
COLORING

Gunkan-maki *are created by*
wrapping a shari *base in* nori
with the ingredients on top.

Unagi *(Freshwater Eel)*

≈ **ORIGIN:** The Shizuoka prefecture of Japan is popular for producing green tea and is home to Mount Fuji, but it's also known for *unagi*, particularly that from Hamanako. China and Korea also export cultivated *unagi*.

👁 **DISTINGUISHING CHARACTERISTICS:** *Unagi* meat is a darker shade of brown than *anago,* and the skin is black to dark gray.

✕ **TASTE & TEXTURE:** *Unagi* has a somewhat plain taste, like that of chicken but with a little bit of fishiness. The flavor is often described as "nutty." *Nigiri unagi* is served warm with *nitsume* over it, adding a barbecue flavor. *Unagi* is popular for the richness of its oils. It has a meaty texture but is nice and soft.

↦ **AVAILABILITY:** *Unagi* is the most popular and widely eaten eel in North America. It is available in most sushi restaurants.

♙ **PRICE:** $$

! **ADDITIONAL INFO:** In Japan, a popular way of having *unagi* is *kabayaki* (barbecue style). The Japanese believe eating freshwater eel gives one strength and stamina. November first is Japan's national *unagi* day. If you have never had sushi, this is one of the things to try.

鰻

BRUSHED WITH
WARM NITSUME

BROWN MEAT

SHARI

BLACK OR DARK
GRAY SKIN

The Japanese eat unagi *to counteract the effects of* natsu-bate
(heat exhaustion).

Sake (Salmon)

≈ **ORIGIN:** *Sake* are cold-water fish that swim in the open ocean and spawn in the fresh water of rivers. In Japan, *sake* are caught in the northern waters of Tohoku, in the northeastern part of the main island, and Hokkaido. The two main types of *sake* are Pacific and Atlantic, and while they are caught in the wild, the trend is toward farming these fish for food.

👁 **DISTINGUISHING CHARACTERISTICS:** *Sake* meat is recognizable by its bright orange color and the white stripes created by the fat. The brighter the meat, the fresher it is.

✂ **TASTE & TEXTURE:** Salmon has a very unique, pleasant fish taste. Its texture is soft and mild, and almost melting, depending on the cut and the amounts of fat and oil.

⟩⟩ **AVAILABILITY:** *Sake* are said to be best in the fall months, but are so popular that they are cultured and are always available at most sushi restaurants.

⌂ **PRICE:** $$

! **ADDITIONAL INFO:** Some of the best-tasting salmon is caught once a year on Alaska's Copper River when the fish are spawning. Copper River salmon are sold in the Pacific Northwest and sometimes make it to markets on the east coast of the U. S. and Canada. The taste experience of this fish is indescribably delicious.

鮭

**FAT FORMS PATTERN
OF WHITE LINES**

SHARI

**BRIGHT
ORANGE MEAT**

*Those who like sake will often
request pieces cut from the belly
because they are rich in oils.*

Ika (Squid, Cuttlefish)

- **Origin:** There are more than 450 kinds of *ika* all over the world, and the name varies depending on the size and shape of the squid. The whole squid—legs, body, ears (the fins on the head), and sometimes even the guts—is used for sushi, but mainly the body is used.

- **Distinguishing Characteristics:** Usually, *ika* is served raw. The color is white and appears translucent. When you get it as a *nimono* item, the skin of the *ika* becomes red and the meat a more solid white, and it is served with *nitsume*.

- **Taste & Texture:** *Ika* tastes plain with a hint of sweetness, and it is chewy and a bit slimy. When it's cooked, it's less slimy but still chewy.

- **Availability:** Although *ika* is not as popular outside of Japan as a sushi item, it is widely available year-round because there are so many different types of *ika* caught all over the world. Chances are your local *sushi-ya* serves *ika*.

- **Price:** $$

- **Additional Info:** *Ika* has a big role in the history of sushi. In the old days, *ika* was one of the main *nimono* items served as *Edomae,* or *nigiri,* sushi. Now that *ika* comes in from all over the world and is available year-round, it is almost always served raw.

CUTS TENDERIZE AND
ORNAMENT THE MEAT

WHITE OR TRANSLUCENT
IN APPEARANCE

SHARI

SHISO ADDS A BIT OF
COLOR AND FLAVOR

Chefs cut ika *meat so that it is
crunchy instead of chewy.*

Uni (Sea Urchin), Bafun Uni (Green Urchin), Murasaki Uni (Purple Urchin)

ORIGIN: *Uni* are found all over the world, but those from cold waters are the best. In Japan, the best *uni* is from Hokkaido. *Uni* are unique because only the ovary is used for sushi. To get to the ovary, the chef cracks open the shell, revealing a tangerine-like body. Then, he or she scoops out the ovary.

DISTINGUISHING CHARACTERISTICS: *Uni* may be different in color—yellow, green, purple, brown, or orange—depending on where they came from and their degree of maturity. Their shape resembles a tongue.

TASTE & TEXTURE: *Uni* tastes like the ocean, with a kind of sweet and salty flavor and a creamy texture.

AVAILABILITY: *Uni* is a standard sushi item and is available most of the year. Nearly every sushi restaurant serves it.

PRICE: $$$$

ADDITIONAL INFO: Tsukiji, the big fish market in Tokyo, carries *uni* from all over the world. It's all available in one big room they call the *uni* room. Much like raw oysters in America, *uni* is a delicacy in Japan. Because the part one eats is the ovary, people in Japan regard *uni* as a giver of energy and stamina.

海胆

COLORS VARY FROM
YELLOW TO BROWN TO ORANGE

NORI

RESEMBLES
A TONGUE

You may get more than one uni per piece of gunkan-maki. *This piece was made from two* uni.

Tako *(Octopus)*

≋ **ORIGIN:** Everyone presumably knows what an octopus looks like: a large head with eight legs. When alive, *tako* will change colors—from red to brown and sometimes even green—to adapt to their environment and camouflage themselves from predators. *Tako* is generally served steamed or boiled, but you might see it raw. *Tako* legs used for sushi can be as long as five feet, and generally these are shipped to restaurants already cooked and packaged. Only the legs are served as sushi.

👁 **DISTINGUISHING CHARACTERISTICS:** *Tako* meat is white with red coloring on the skin when it is cooked. Depending on the cut, you may also see the *kyu ban* (tentacles).

✕ **TASTE & TEXTURE:** *Tako* has a slightly oceanic flavor, with a subtle sweetness that comes out as you eat it. It is on the chewy side, but can be very tender, depending on the cut and the section of the leg. Make sure it's very fresh if you're having it raw.

)⊃ **AVAILABILITY:** Like *ika,* *tako* is available in sushi restaurants almost everywhere.

△ **PRICE:** $$

! **ADDITIONAL INFO:** *Tako* is called the "devil fish" and it's not very popular around the world, maybe because it has eight legs and resembles a spider. In Asia, *tako* is a delicacy enjoyed in many different ways.

RED COLORING
FROM SKIN

NORI BELT

WHITE MEAT

SHARI

"U" SHAPE FROM
CIRCULAR TENTACLES

Tako is generally served cooked, but if you do have it raw, the meat should be moving when you eat it.

Inari-Zushi
(Tofu Pouches Filled with Rice)

⚌ **ORIGIN:** To make these, a chef deep-fries a tofu pouch, cooks it in soy sauce, and fills it with rice. *Inari-zushi* is a long-time favorite in Japan. It is a common food made at home and it is traditionally shared with others as a gesture of goodwill.

👁 **DISTINGUISHING CHARACTERISTICS:** These are little brown pouches stuffed with rice. The size may vary depending on who makes them.

✕ **TASTE & TEXTURE:** The taste of *inari-zushi* is a mixture of flavors. First, there is the sweet soy sauce with the taste of the deep-fried tofu, then the vinegar-seasoned sushi rice. All of this together creates the harmony of *inari-zushi*. It is very soft and mild in one's mouth.

⮑ **AVAILABILITY:** This should be available everywhere. If you don't see it on the menu, just ask for it, because any sushi chef will know of it.

△ **PRICE:** $

! **ADDITIONAL INFO:** Oinari-san is the name of a Japanese god for which there are many shrines in Japan. Small statues of foxes protect these shrines, and it is said the favorite food of the foxes is *abura-age*—the deep-fried tofu pouches. The name *inari-zushi* is taken from Oinari-san and the practice of leaving food at the shrine as an offering to bring one good luck and safe passage.

BROWN COLORING FROM
COOKING IN SOY SAUCE

稲荷

SHARI INSIDE

Inari-zushi *is an excellent way to introduce
children to sushi because it is sweet.*

Tamago (*Eggs and Fish Roe*) *Different Types of Eggs and Their Role in Sushi*

....

Tamago—sushi omelet—is one of the basic items in sushi and is used in literally every sushi restaurant in the world. Fish eggs, or roe, are also used in every sushi restaurant in some form or another. In Japan, roe is very popular, and a wide variety, from various fish, are available. Elsewhere in the sushi world, roe is less popular, but those who enjoy sushi usually experiment with and come to enjoy eating roe just as the Japanese do. Once you are ready for the full sushi experience, make sure you include roe as part of your adventuring.

玉
子

Ikura (*Salmon Roe*)

≈ **ORIGIN:** Most of the *ikura* used for sushi in North America comes from Alaska, and sometimes from Canada. Much of it is exported to Japan.

👁 **DISTINGUISHING CHARACTERISTICS:** These eggs are reddish-orange in color and very shiny, like little red jewels.

🗑 **PRESENTATION:** These will most often be served as *gunkan-maki,* or "battleship sushi," in which the rice is wrapped with seaweed and topped with *ikura*.

✂ **TASTE & TEXTURE:** The taste of *ikura* is salty. They are very soft and burst easily in the mouth. Because they are oily, they taste and feel very creamy.

🗘 **AVAILABILITY:** Even though salmon spawn only once a year or less, their eggs are salted and frozen by a number of suppliers, so they are available year-round in most sushi restaurants.

🛆 **PRICE:** $$$

! **ADDITIONAL INFO:** *Ikura* taken at the beginning of the salmon's spawning season are considered to be the best because the skin of the eggs is thin and that makes them gentle. Eggs taken at the end of the season have a thicker skin that may linger in the mouth. In Japan, *ikura* are popular among all age groups from the elderly to the very young, even babies.

REDDISH-ORANGE
COLORING

SHAPED LIKE
SMALL JEWELS

イクラ

SHARI INSIDE

NORI

Ikura *are often used as an additional ingredient because they add
creaminess to any item.*

Tamago (*Sushi Omelet*)

≋ **ORIGIN:** *Tamago* is made using the same chicken eggs that are used commonly throughout the world. To prepare it, a chef will take a number of eggs and mix them with *dashi* (fish-based soup), salt, sugar, and a bit of sake, and cook them into a loaf.

👁 **DISTINGUISHING CHARACTERISTICS:** *Tamago* is always yellow, and you will see it cut into rectangular pieces.

🍥 **PRESENTATION:** The most common way you will see *tamago* served is *nigiri*-style on top of rice with a nori belt. You may also see it used as an edible decoration for a larger dish, in rolls such as *futo-maki* (see page 152), used as a garnish, or served sashimi-style.

✂ **TASTE & TEXTURE:** *Tamago* is a sweet, custardlike omelet. Every chef has his own recipe, so the flavors will differ slightly from place to place.

⤳ **AVAILABILITY:** This is a standard sushi item that is served everywhere.

🅐 **PRICE:** $

! **ADDITIONAL INFO:** *Tamago* was traditionally made in the *atsu-yaki* style, in which ground shrimp is mixed into the egg to add thickness and richer taste. In Japan, it is said that trying *tamago* is a way of testing the chef's skill.

玉子

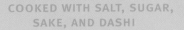

NORI BELT

SHARI

This standard item is available to sushi restaurants pre-made, but true sushi chefs always make their own.

Tobbiko, Tobiuo-Noko
(Flying Fish Roe)

ORIGIN: The *tobiuo* (flying fish) is not used for sushi itself, because the flavor is bland and lacks the richness of other sushi items. In Japan, flying fish are usually dried and cooked over an open flame. *Tobbiko*, however, are taken from the fish and prepared for sale to restaurants in half-pound boxes.

DISTINGUISHING CHARACTERISTICS: These are tiny eggs that look like caviar, but are red to orange in color. Green *wasabi tobbiko* is also produced by seafood sellers.

PRESENTATION: Like *ikura*, these will be served in the *gunkan-maki* style, sometimes with a quail egg on top. They are also used in various rolls to add color.

TASTE & TEXTURE: *Tobbiko* are salty and crunchy. They burst in your mouth as you chew them. *Wasabi tobbiko* are spicy.

AVAILABILITY: Our *tobbiko* come from Japan. These are available year-round at nearly every sushi restaurant.

PRICE: $$

ADDITIONAL INFO: *Tobbiko gunkan-maki* is often served with a quail egg (*uzura*) on top. To prepare it in this style, the chef will create a small pit in the *tobbiko* and place the *uzura* yolk in the center.

GREEN TOBBIKO GETS
COLOR AND SPICINESS FROM
SOAKING IN WASABI

TOBBIKO IS
GENERALLY RED
TO ORANGE

飛子

NORI

SHARI INSIDE

*Some creative chefs use both colors
of* tobbiko *and a quail egg to create
a* gunkan-maki *called a "stoplight."*

Kazunoko (Herring Roe)

≋ **ORIGIN:** Herring come from the cold waters of northern Japan, Alaska, Canada, and Norway. Their roe are held in a sack within the belly of the female fish, and these sacks are used for sushi.

👁 **DISTINGUISHING CHARACTERISTICS:** The egg sack these tiny eggs come in is very firm. The roe are yellow and the sacks are usually four to five inches in length and are shaped like a finger.

🍣 **PRESENTATION:** *Kazunoko* are usually served *nigiri*-style, sometimes topped with bonito flakes (*katsu-bushi*), although some people may enjoy these as a sashimi side dish with a bit of sake.

✂ **TASTE & TEXTURE:** These are generally marinated in a salt-and-sake mixture, so you will taste these flavors first, but as you bite into *kazunoko,* a fishy flavor is released. The roe are very crunchy, and the sack is so firm that you can literally break it in half.

🌤 **AVAILABILITY:** Winter is the best season to enjoy *kazunoko,* because the fish spawn in fall and winter. Generally you will see these more during the wintertime, and they will be available at many *sushi-ya* throughout the sushi world.

🏷 **PRICE:** $$$

❗ **ADDITIONAL INFO:** In Japan, *kazunoko* is said to bring good fortune; it is often served at New Year's festivities to bring good luck for the coming year.

数の子

RIGID EGG
SACK

BONITO FLAKES

LIGHT YELLOW
EGGS

NORI BELT

SHARI

SHAPED LIKE
A FINGER

Bonito flakes are shaved off of
preserved and dried pieces of bonito
that are nearly rock hard.

Tarako *(Cod Roe, Pollock Roe)*

≈ **ORIGIN:** *Tarako* are the roe taken from cod or pollock. These roe come in a small sack shaped like a finger, usually between three to four inches long.

👁 **DISTINGUISHING CHARACTERISTICS:** The color of these eggs ranges from pink to light red, and the sack is transparent.

🍥 **PRESENTATION:** These will most often be served *nigiri*-style, but the chef may also open the sack and scrape the eggs out to use in *maki-mono*.

✄ **TASTE & TEXTURE:** As with other fish eggs, the flavor of *tarako* is salty, but they also have a slight fishy taste. They are soft and pasty in texture and can be a fun challenge to eat if you've never tried them before.

⤜ **AVAILABILITY:** This is not a popular item in North America, so you only see this at a *sushi-ya* every once in a while. In Asia, however, this is a very well-known sushi item you can get almost anywhere.

💰 **PRICE:** $$

! **ADDITIONAL INFO:** In Japan, *tarako* are used often in *onigiri* (wrapped rice balls) or *ochazuke* (tea over rice), which is a traditional dish. Even though the U. S. is the largest exporter of *tarako* to Asia, there is only a very small market for it here. Seattle, Washington, is the biggest port in the world for buying and selling *tarako*.

THOUSANDS OF TINY
EGGS MAKE UP
A PIECE OF SUSHI

TRANSPARENT SACK
HOLDS EGGS TOGETHER

SHARI

COLOR RANGES FROM
PINK TO RED

Like ankimo *and* tobbiko, tarako
*are served as sushi even though cod
is not.*

Komochi Konbu, Kazunoko Konbu, Komochi Wakame
(Herring Roe on Kelp and Seaweed)

ORIGIN: During spawning, female herring lay their eggs on kelp leaves or seaweed, and the male herring come around and release their sperm onto the eggs, which causes the eggs to firm up and stick to the kelp or seaweed. The leaves are then cut away by harvesters, with the eggs intact, and this is what is served as *komochi konbu* or *wakame*.

DISTINGUISHING CHARACTERISTICS: *Komochi konbu* and *wakame* look like leaves with a blanket of yellow herring roe on both sides.

PRESENTATION: The large leaves are cut into little pieces and served *nigiri*-style or as sashimi.

TASTE & TEXTURE: The taste is like the ocean, a bit salty with a slight bitterness in the flavor from the kelp or seaweed. The texture is crunchy.

AVAILABILITY: In Japan, *komochi konbu* is a delicacy, but it is not popular in North America and is only served occasionally.

PRICE: $$$$

ADDITIONAL INFO: As with *kazunoko*, eating *komochi konbu* and *wakame* is said to bring good luck because the roe represent vitality and new life.

鯑の子

SEAWEED

BONITO FLAKES

NORI BELT

HERRING EGGS

SHARI

The highest quality komochi konbu has a thick layer of eggs on both sides of the seaweed.

Masago (*Smelt Roe*)

≋ **ORIGIN:** *Masago* are tiny eggs like *tobbiko,* and some *sushi-ya* may serve *masago* instead of *tobbiko.*

👁 **DISTINGUISHING CHARACTERISTICS:** These look like bright orange caviar, just like *tobbiko.*

🍣 **PRESENTATION:** *Masago* are served as a *gunkan-maki,* and are also used as decorative garnish for *maki-mono,* sashimi, and *nigiri-zushi.*

✂ **TASTE & TEXTURE:** The flavor and feel of *masago* are just like *tobbiko*—they are virtually interchangeable.

⤳ **AVAILABILITY:** *Masago* usually come from Japan, but there are other places around the world that produce them. Some of the *masago* available in the United States comes from Iceland. Since *masago* and *tobbiko* are virtually the same item used for the same things, many places will have one or the other.

⌂ **PRICE:** $$

! **ADDITIONAL INFO:** Cod roe (*tarako*), shrimp roe (*ebiko*), or crab roe (*kaniko*), are also used as a substitute for *tobikko* or *masago.*

SMELT ROE

真子

NORI

SHARI INSIDE

This alternative to tobbiko is often used as a garnish because it is stickier.

Maki-Mono (Rolls)
The Most Popular and Common Rolls

....

Rolls have been around for a very long time in sushi, their origins dating back hundreds of years to the period when Kyoto was the political capital of Japan.

There are three styles of *maki-mono* served today. *Hoso-maki-zushi,* or thin roll sushi, is made by rolling *shari* and one or two ingredients in a half-sheet of nori. *Futo-maki-zushi,* or large roll sushi, uses a full sheet of nori, allowing a number of ingredients to be rolled together. *Ura-maki-zushi* is a style in which the half-sheet of nori is on the inside of the roll between the *shari* and the fish or other ingredients at the very center. These are referred to as "inside-out" rolls in English, and are the most popular style of roll served in North America. The ubiquitous California roll is made in this style.

Te-maki-zushi, or hand-rolled sushi, is probably the newest style of *maki-mono.* It started as a quick snack made by and for sushi chefs as they worked. To make it, they grab a half-sheet of nori, put a little sushi rice onto it, add some tuna or yellowtail or whatever other ingredients they want, quickly roll the seaweed into a cone in their hands, and eat it.

巻き物

Tekka-Maki *(Tuna Roll)*

≈ **ORIGIN:** *Tekka-maki* is a basic item that has been around roughly two hundred years, since the Edo period.

▽ **INGREDIENTS:** Nori, *shari*, wasabi, and *akami*. You can also request a roll made with *chutoro, toro,* or *otoro.*

⊟ **PRESENTATION:** *Tekka-maki* is commonly served as a *hoso-maki*. A small bit of wasabi is added between the rice and tuna. *Tekka-maki* appears dark green or black on the outside, and the raw tuna gives it a red center.

✂ **TASTE & TEXTURE:** The taste of tuna combines excellently with rice and seaweed. None of the flavors are too strong, and the result is a simple roll that is great for dipping in soy sauce and is uncomplicated to the palate.

♤ **PRICE:** $$

! **ADDITIONAL INFO:** *Tekka-maki* gets its name from a gambling place called Tekka-Ba. Gamblers wanted something to eat without getting their hands messy, so the chefs created the simple but delicious tuna roll and named it after the gambling spot.

AKAMI MAGURO

SHARI

鉄火巻

NORI OUTSIDE

Tekka-maki, *a simple roll, is a great item to use to introduce children to* maki-mono.

Kappa-Maki *(Cucumber Roll)*

≈ **ORIGIN:** *Kappa-maki* is another basic sushi item that has been around a long time. Traditionally these were made by rolling a whole thin Japanese cucumber into the center of a roll. Now you are likely to see this served with regular cucumber at the center. This roll is a popular one with kids and is a good introduction to sushi for people who are not used to raw fish.

▽ **INGREDIENTS:** Nori, *shari,* sesame seeds, wasabi, and cucumber.

⬠ **PRESENTATION:** This is made as a *hoso-maki,* so it will be fairly thin. It's black on the outside and white on the inside, with a green center.

✂ **TASTE & TEXTURE:** The taste is a mixture of seaweed, rice, and cucumber. You will also taste the sesame slightly, as it adds a bit of a smoky flavor. The texture is on the crunchy side because of the cucumber.

⌂ **PRICE:** $

! **ADDITIONAL INFO:** *Kappa-maki* got its name from a fictional creature called Kappa that is said to live in swampy areas and is green with a flat top. *Kappa-maki,* when cut, has a flat, green top.

CUCUMBER

SESAME
SEEDS

SHARI

河童巻

NORI OUTSIDE

Instead of large chunks of cucumber a chef might julienne a cucumber to enhance the texture and appearance of kappa maki.

Kampyo-Maki *(Gourd Roll)*

≈ **ORIGIN:** *Kampyo* is a vegetable that has been used in Japan for a long time. It is sold dried in long strips. Chefs prepare it by softening it in water for several hours and then cooking it in a soy-based broth.

▽ **INGREDIENTS:** Nori, *shari,* wasabi, and *kampyo.*

▣ **PRESENTATION:** *Kampyo-maki* is a *hoso-maki.* The *kampyo* turns brown when it is cooked, so this roll is black on the outside, white on the inside, and has a brown center.

✂ **TASTE & TEXTURE:** The taste of *kampyo-maki* is a pleasant, mellow, sweet soy flavor. When the gourd is cooked it softens, so this roll will feel very soft in your mouth.

♨ **PRICE:** $

! **ADDITIONAL INFO:** *Kampyo* is often used creatively in Japanese cooking—a chef might use it to hold things together, or cook strips of *kampyo* in various broths and then use the *kampyo* as multicolored garnish. It is also added to other rolls such as *futo-maki* (see page 152) or vegetarian rolls (see page 178).

KAMPYO IS BROWN FROM
COOKING IN SOY BROTH

SHARI

NORI OUTSIDE

Whereas many maki-mono *are cut into six or eight
pieces,* kampyo-maki *is usually cut into four
longer segments.*

California Roll

≈ **ORIGIN:** This sushi creation has a "Made in America" stamp on it. The avocado is a big product of California. Every U. S. sushi restaurant has its own version of the California roll.

🍶 **INGREDIENTS:** Nori, *shari,* avocado, *kani,* and often sesame seeds, cucumber, and *tobbiko*.

🥣 **PRESENTATION:** California rolls are served as an *ura-maki,* so they are white on the outside, though a chef might cover these in *tobbiko,* giving them an orange exterior. Inside this roll is crab, avocado, and perhaps some cucumber or another vegetable. *Tobbiko* is often included inside with the crab and avocado for color, and cucumber can be added to give the roll a little more texture and crunch.

✂ **TASTE & TEXTURE:** The match of avocado with crab is excellent—creamy because of the avocado, sweet due to the crab flavor. The softness of the avocado and the meatiness of the crab are great together.

🥢 **PRICE:** $$

! **ADDITIONAL INFO:** This item is the number-one seller in America and is an excellent item for people who are first learning about sushi.

TOBBIKO

CRAB

AVOCADO

カルフォニヤ巻

SESAME
SEEDS

CUCUMBER

SHARI

Although the pictured roll has tobbiko on the inside, chefs will often roll this in roe, coating the outside.

Oshinko-Maki (Pickle Roll)

≋ **ORIGIN:** *Oshinko-maki* generally uses pickled daikon radish. Farmers salt and dry the radish to soften it up, and then pickle it in sweet vinegar. *Oshinko* is used not only for *maki,* but also as a side dish in sushi.

▽ **INGREDIENTS:** Nori, *shari,* wasabi, sesame seeds, and *oshinko*.

⬡ **PRESENTATION:** *Oshinko-maki* is made in the *hoso-maki* style. It's black on the outside and white on the inside. The center might be yellow or white, depending on the way the radish was pickled. At times other types of pickled vegetables are used, so the center of the roll might be orange, brown, or purple.

✂ **TASTE & TEXTURE:** The taste is usually a bit salty with a slight sweetness. The pickle goes well with the rice and seaweed. The texture of *oshinko-maki* is slightly crunchy.

△ **PRICE:** $

! **ADDITIONAL INFO:** This a traditional roll, particularly popular with Asian people because of the pickled radish. The Japanese eat pickled vegetables as a side dish at almost every meal. There are even specialty stores that sell all different types of pickled vegetables.

DEPENDING ON THE PICKLED
VEGETABLE, CENTER MIGHT BE
ORANGE, BROWN, OR PURPLE

SESAME SEEDS

YELLOW PICKLED
DAIKON RADISH

NORI OUTSIDE

Yama-gobo, *or burdock root, is another popular pickled item that is used in* oshinko-maki.

Spicy Tuna Roll

≈ **ORIGIN:** This mixture of tuna, spices, and mayonnaise is an American creation owing to the use of mayonnaise in the United States. Chefs in Japan have begun serving this roll, and it is becoming popular there.

▽ **INGREDIENTS:** Every place has its own recipe for this roll. The basic ingredients are mayonnaise, soy sauce, and a chile oil called *rayu*. Small amounts of these items are mixed with the tuna, some sesame seeds, and a bit of chopped scallion. It is then rolled with *shari,* nori, and a little wasabi.

🍵 **PRESENTATION:** This roll usually comes as an *ura-maki*, so it is white on the outside with the black line of the seaweed surrounding the reddish or white (if albacore is used) tuna mixture in the center.

✂ **TASTE & TEXTURE:** The tuna and mayonnaise give this a creamy and tangy flavor, and the spiciness is generally fairly mild. This is a soft roll, although there may be a bit of a crunch if the chef used scallion in the tuna mixture.

△ **PRICE:** $$$

! **ADDITIONAL INFO:** This is a great roll for anyone who loves tuna. You can also ask for spicy tuna as a *te-maki* or *hoso-maki*.

スパイス 鮪巻

MIXTURE OF TUNA,
MAYONNAISE, CHILE OIL,
SCALLION, SOY SAUCE

SHARI OUTSIDE

SESAME SEEDS

It is common for other types of fish to be served with this spicy sauce recipe.

Ume-Shiso-Maki *(Sour Plum Paste with Beefsteak Leaf Roll)*

ORIGIN: *Umeboshi* (sour plum paste) is made from plums that are picked and pickled before they ripen. To make *umeboshi,* pickled plums are soaked in brine with red *shiso* leaves, which gives them their pinkish color. The fruit is then processed to produce the paste. *Shiso* is the jagged leaf of the beefsteak plant, which is part of the mint and basil family.

INGREDIENTS: Nori, *shari, shiso,* and *umeboshi.*

PRESENTATION: The plum paste is pinkish-purple or sometimes orange in color, and the *shiso* is green. This is prepared in the *hoso-maki* style.

TASTE & TEXTURE: Since *umeboshi* and *shiso* are such important items in Japanese cuisine, tasting this roll is like tasting Japan. The sourness of the plum paste and the basil-like flavor of the beefsteak leaves can be an acquired taste, but this traditional soft and sour roll is quite excellent.

PRICE: $

ADDITIONAL INFO: Some people like to finish their meals with this roll in order to leave a refreshing taste in their mouths. *Umeboshi* is extremely popular in Japan as one of the main condiments in its cuisine. Many people eat it for breakfast.

SHISO
LEAVES

SHARI

SESAME
SEEDS

SOUR PLUM
PASTE

NORI OUTSIDE

ウメシソ巻

*Chefs often serve this as the last item in a chef's choice
or between courses as a palate cleanser.*

Spider Roll

ORIGIN: This, yet again, is a U. S. creation. It is likely that Japanese sushi chefs on the east coast of the United States originated this roll because the blue, or soft-shell, crab is native to that area.

INGREDIENTS: Nori, *shari,* fried soft-shell crab legs, avocado, cucumber, sesame seeds, *tobbiko,* and *kaiware* (radish sprouts).

PRESENTATION: The spider roll is an *ura-maki*, and usually comes with the crab legs sticking out of the roll to make it look like a spider. Often avocado and *tobbiko* are used in the center of this roll to add to the flavor and to enhance its appearance.

TASTE & TEXTURE: The flavor is like a mixture of a crab sandwich and crab salad with rice. The texture is on the crunchy side because the crab is deep-fried.

PRICE: $$$

ADDITIONAL INFO: Spider rolls have become a very standard item served in U. S. *sushi-ya*, and you may see this served with a number of different ingredients accompanying the crab legs in the center of it.

FRIED SOFT-SHELL
CRAB LEGS

KAIWARE

TOBBIKO

AVOCADO

NORI

SESAME

SHARI OUTSIDE

CUCUMBER

スパイダ巻

Kaiware are added to spider rolls because they enhance the presentation.

Avocado-Maki (Avocado Roll)

≈ **ORIGIN:** Like the California roll, the avocado-*maki* is the result of sushi's growing popularity in the United States, and the availability of avocado to sushi chefs. This is a new take on the basic, traditional Japanese rolls in the *hoso-maki* style, such as *tekka-maki* and *kappa-maki*.

▽ **INGREDIENTS:** Nori, *shari,* sesame seeds, wasabi, and avocado.

▣ **PRESENTATION:** This roll is black on the outside and white on the inside, with a green center. The sesame seeds are mixed into the rice.

✕ **TASTE & TEXTURE:** As *maki-mono* go, this roll is on the simple side. If you like avocado, you will like this roll, because avocado is the main flavor. Avocado-*maki* is soft and creamy.

⌂ **PRICE:** $

! **ADDITIONAL INFO:** While avocado is widely used for sushi in North America and people here often think of it as a main ingredient in sushi, this fruit is used very little for sushi in Japan, although its popularity is starting to increase there.

SESAME
SEEDS

AVOCADO

NORI OUTSIDE

アボカド巻き

This is a very healthy roll because avocado contains non-saturated or "good" fats.

Negi Hama-Maki
(Yellowtail with Scallion Roll)

≋ **ORIGIN:** This roll is a Japanese invention. The style of mixing the fish and scallions together is used very widely in Japan. The flavor of the onions counteracts the fishy smell often present in richer fish such as yellowtail, allowing people to concentrate on the flavor of the fish.

▽ **INGREDIENTS:** Nori, *shari,* wasabi, sesame seeds, scallions, and *hamachi*.

◱ **PRESENTATION:** Usually this is served as an *ura-maki,* so it is white on the outside, and tan and green on the inside.

✂ **TASTE & TEXTURE:** If you like *hamachi,* you will love this roll. The taste of the yellowtail is greatly enhanced by the addition of scallion for a great harmony of flavors.

⌂ **PRICE:** $$

! **ADDITIONAL INFO:** Although you will often see scallion combined with *hamachi,* many other rich-flavored fish are served in this style. If you like it, try scallions with different fish such as *maguro* or *karei*.

YELLOWTAIL

SCALLION

NORI

ネギハマ巻

SESAME SEEDS

SHARI OUTSIDE

This roll is served in the hoso-maki *style at* sushi-ya *in Japan. The "inside out" style is not widely used there for any rolls.*

Futo-Maki (Large Roll, Fat Roll)

≋ **ORIGIN:** *Futo-maki,* one of the basic rolls, has been around for over two hundred years. It is very popular in Japan and is traditionally served at family functions or celebrations such as New Year's because it is so colorful and hearty.

▽ **INGREDIENTS:** Nori, *shari, tamago,* wasabi, *oboro* (sweet fish powder), and a number of cooked or pickled vegetables and sometimes fish.

⌣ **PRESENTATION:** This roll is served with the seaweed on the outside, like a giant sushi burrito.

✕ **TASTE & TEXTURE:** As rolls go, this is going to be one of the most complex combinations of flavors and textures, due to the number of ingredients. Ask the chef what goes into his *futo-maki.* The texture can be soft, chewy, or crunchy, depending on what is inside.

△ **PRICE:** $$$

! **ADDITIONAL INFO:** There is a variation of the *futo-maki* style called *date-maki* or "dandy-rolls" due to their variety of colors and their showiness. *Date-maki* is essentially a *futo-maki* rolled in *tamago,* although the ingredients inside may vary slightly from those traditionally found in *futo-maki.* These rolls are not served often, but remain a popular treat for special occasions in Japan.

TAMAGO

SHARI

OBORO INSIDE

NORI OUTSIDE

PICKLED AND COOKED
VEGETABLES

太巻

Oboro *is used in sushi only for* futo-maki. *Some people ask for oboro on the side and enjoy its sweet flavor.*

Una-Kyu-Maki
(Eel and Cucumber Roll)

≈ | **ORIGIN:** This traditional roll is a Japanese product that caters to the people there who really enjoy *unagi*.

▽ | **INGREDIENTS:** Nori, *shari,* wasabi, sesame seeds, *unagi,* and cucumber.

🍥 | **PRESENTATION:** This roll is served inside out, with the rice on the outside and the *unagi* and cucumber inside. Often this will have *nitsume* served over the top of it, adding a brown color to the mix.

✄ | **TASTE & TEXTURE:** This roll has a very strong *unagi* flavor, especially when it's served with *nitsume*. The soft eel with the fresh, crunchy cucumber makes an excellent combination of textures.

⚖ | **PRICE:** $$

! | **ADDITIONAL INFO:** *Una-kyu-maki* is a popular roll because the eel is cooked and the flavor is sweet, like a teriyaki flavor. I think this is a great roll for people who are scared to try anything new. I tell novice sushi eaters to try it because *unagi* tastes like chicken. They usually like it and begin to explore other sushi items.

NORI

CUCUMBER

AVOCADO

LIGHT BROWN
UNAGI MEAT

うなぎ巻

SESAME SEEDS

SHARI OUTSIDE

Not traditionally used in this roll, chefs may choose to include avocado to add richness and creaminess.

Te-Maki (Hand Roll)

~ **ORIGIN:** *Te-maki* was invented at the sushi counter by chefs who needed a quick meal that they could eat while they worked.

▽ **INGREDIENTS:** You can generally ask for any *hoso-maki* or *ura-maki* roll on the menu to be made in this style. Most chefs will also let you choose your own ingredients.

▣ **PRESENTATION:** *Te-maki* is shaped like a cone, with the different ingredients emerging from its top like colorful flowers from a bouquet.

✄ **TASTE & TEXTURE:** The flavors will vary with the ingredients.

♙ **PRICE:** Varies with ingredients.

! **ADDITIONAL INFO:** When you get your hand roll, you should eat it right away before the seaweed gets moist from the rice and becomes chewy. *Te-maki* are very popular because they allow you to have a taste of the flavors of certain rolls without having to order the whole roll. If you want to try something you've never had, try it in the *te-maki* style. This will allow you to sample the flavors and judge your interest.

CONE-SHAPED NORI

SHARI AND OTHER
INGREDIENTS

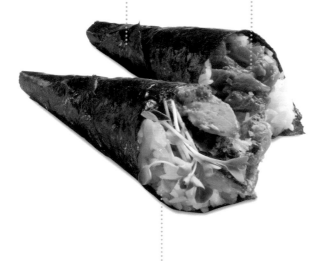

ASK FOR ANY ROLL IN THIS STYLE
OR CREATE YOUR OWN

A skilled sushi chef can often roll te-maki *using
only one hand.*

手巻き

Sake-Maki *(Salmon Roll)*

ORIGIN: This is a traditionally Japanese preparation in which the fish is mixed with scallions to add a bit of kick to the flavor of the roll, but the use of *sake* is the result of sushi's popularity outside of Japan, in areas where salmon are caught fresh locally.

INGREDIENTS: Nori, *shari, sake,* wasabi, scallions, sesame seeds, and cucumber.

PRESENTATION: This is an *ura-maki* that looks like the *hinomaru*: the Japanese flag.

TASTE & TEXTURE: The texture is pleasant, and the taste changes depending on what kind of salmon is used. We use smoked salmon with some cucumber and scallion for a strong salmon flavor. Other sushi restaurants may use raw salmon for a mellower taste.

PRICE: $$

ADDITIONAL INFO: Another roll using *sake* that you may see is the "salmon skin roll," in which grilled salmon skin is the main ingredient. This may sound a bit unappealing, but it is actually very popular because salmon skin is quite tasty.

BRIGHT ORANGE SAKE

SCALLION

CUCUMBER

SHARI OUTSIDE

SESAME SEEDS

Sake is also great mixed with the same sauce as that on the spicy tuna roll (see page 142).

Creative Rolls
Examples of How Local Ingredients Have Inspired Chefs

One of the greatest things about sushi's growing popularity is the number of different ingredients available to chefs all over the world, and the variety of tastes and flavors that people from different areas of the globe enjoy. The result has been an escalation in the creativity of sushi chefs as they combine the tastes of the world into their cuisine. This creativity is perhaps most evident in the development of *maki-mono*.

In the following pages I've included a few of the creative rolls that have caught on, along with a few of the rolls I've created in my time as a chef. I encourage you to try the rolls that are particular to the *sushi-ya* you are visiting, so you can appreciate the artistry and skill of the chef.

独
創
的

Caterpillar Roll

ORIGIN: As we have seen with other rolls using avocado, this was developed by sushi chefs in America. Avocado is still rare in Japan, but people are starting to enjoy it more and more.

INGREDIENTS: The ingredients that make this a caterpillar roll are avocado and *nitsume*. What comes on the inside of the roll will vary depending on the chef. We use eel and cucumber on the inside of our caterpillar roll.

PRESENTATION: This *ura-maki* roll resembles a caterpillar because of the green color of the avocado along with the brown of the *nitsume*.

TASTE & TEXTURE: The avocado and *nitsume* add a creamy texture and sweet flavor that make almost any roll better.

PRICE: $$$

ADDITIONAL INFO: Because of this roll's popularity in the U. S., most sushi chefs throughout the world will know how to make a caterpillar roll, even if it isn't on the menu. Ask your local chef about it if you don't see it.

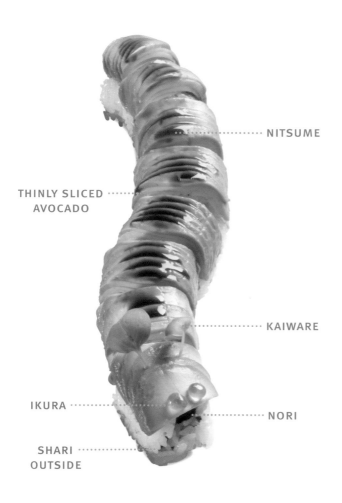

NITSUME

THINLY SLICED
AVOCADO

KAIWARE

IKURA

NORI

SHARI
OUTSIDE

巻キャタピラ

*The insides of a caterpillar roll vary with the chef, as
will the amount of creativity put into the appearance.*

California Crunch

ORIGIN: The "crunch" is a new fusion style of *maki-mono*. Many *sushi-ya* have some type of crunch roll. We took the popular California roll and made it a bit better by adding *temp-kasu* (tempura crumbs) to give it a crunch.

INGREDIENTS: California roll plus tempura crumbs. Tempura crumbs are made from deep-fried tempura batter. Recipes for tempura batter will vary, but flour, cornstarch, eggs, baking powder, and water are the main ingredients, with spices added to enhance the flavor.

PRESENTATION: The tempura crumbs on the outside give this roll a light brown to golden yellow color, with the green of avocado, the orange of *tobbiko,* and the milky color of crabmeat decorating the center.

TASTE & TEXTURE: The taste and texture of this roll are amazing! The *temp-kasu* enhance the flavor of the crab and make the roll crunch as you eat it.

PRICE: $$

ADDITIONAL INFO: This roll was a hit from the day it got on the menu. As a chef, sometimes you don't know if your new creations will sell, but when people like it enough to order another, you know it's good. You will see tempura vegetables or shrimp tempura used in a number of rolls these days, and you may also see entire rolls coated in tempura batter and deep-fried.

AVOCADO

CRAB

SESAME SEEDS

LIGHT BROWN
TEMPURA CRUMBS

カルフォニャ
クランチ

*This roll has the crunch of tempura but is healthier
than many other tempura rolls because it uses
less batter.*

Yokozuna-Maki
(Grand Champion Roll)

≈ | **ORIGIN:** I created this roll for myself while I was training for sumo. I used to have this enormous roll for dinner once a week.

▽ | **INGREDIENTS:** Nori, *shari, tobikko,* wasabi, and six to eight different types of seafood.

◻ | **PRESENTATION:** The *yokozuna* roll is made in the *futo-maki* style, with a whole sheet of seaweed enclosing the mass of ingredients. Inside this roll a variety of seafood is used, so the colors might be a mixture of red, white, orange, brown, and green. I also use *tobbiko* to add to the appearance.

✂ | **TASTE & TEXTURE:** The taste and texture of this roll are amazing. Some parts are soft, some chewy, all inside your mouth at once. The flavor of all of the different items together is very good, especially with a bit of soy.

△ | **PRICE:** $$$

! | **ADDITIONAL INFO:** I named this roll after the ultimate goal of the sumo wrestler: to be the *yokozuna* (grand champion) at sumo tournaments.

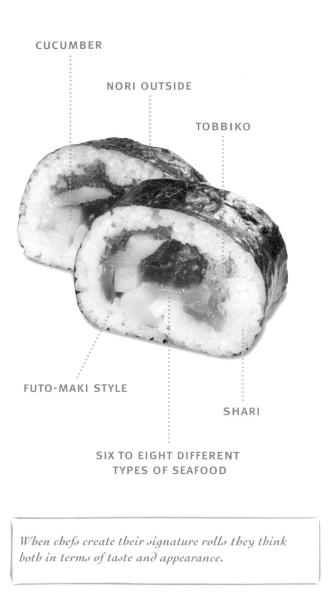

CUCUMBER

NORI OUTSIDE

TOBBIKO

横綱巻

FUTO-MAKI STYLE

SHARI

SIX TO EIGHT DIFFERENT
TYPES OF SEAFOOD

*When chefs create their signature rolls they think
both in terms of taste and appearance.*

Rainbow Roll

ORIGIN: This is a creative roll that originated in Japan. The many different types of fish used for the rainbow roll give it its name.

INGREDIENTS: Nori, *shari,* wasabi, and one or two other ingredients in the center of the roll, along with a variety of fish.

PRESENTATION: This *ura-maki* has a variety of fish wrapped over the outside of it. There is great beauty in the colorful arrangement of the fish, and how it's cut and presented. The ingredients on the inside are generally very simple, so the focus is on the fish.

TASTE & TEXTURE: The taste and texture change with each bite, as different fish combine with the filling of the roll.

PRICE: $$$

ADDITIONAL INFO: Beautiful to look at and great-tasting, this roll is popular nearly everywhere. The name might differ, depending on where you are. Don't hesitate to ask the chef if he or she serves a rainbow roll—everyone knows how to make this.

DIFFERENT TYPES OF FISH MAKE THIS
ROLL A RAINBOW OF COLORS

レンボー巻き

SHARI OUTSIDE

INGREDIENTS ON THE INSIDE VARY;
HERE YOU SEE CRAB AND AVOCADO

The key to creating a great rainbow roll is not the variety of fish, but the variety of colors.

Vegetarian Sushi
Delicious Items for the Veggie-Lover

One of the major reasons sushi has become so popular worldwide is that it is healthy. People who do not eat red meat enjoy sushi because it is based entirely on seafood. And even those who do not eat meat at all can find great vegetarian options at a *sushi-ya*.

This section covers some of the vegetarian items most commonly found, but certainly these will differ from restaurant to restaurant. A number of vegetarian options have also already been mentioned in previous sections, so be sure to look for *inari-zushi* (see page 112), *kappa-maki* (page 134), *kampyo-maki* (see page 136), *oshinko-maki* (see page 140), *ume-shiso-maki* (see page 144), and avocado-*maki* (see page 148) at your local *sushi-ya*.

ベゲタリアン

Avocado Nigiri

≈ **ORIGIN:** Avocado *nigiri* was developed by an American sushi chef as a vegetarian item. Avocados are packed with vitamins, nutrients, and are extremely low in saturated fats. They are among the healthiest fruits you can eat, so their prominent role in sushi restaurants outside of Japan has added another very healthy aspect to this cuisine.

▽ **INGREDIENTS:** This is a simple sushi item—one or two slices of avocado over *shari* with a little nori belt.

✕ **TASTE & TEXTURE:** The texture of the creamy avocado with the sushi rice is simple and delicious.

△ **PRICE:** $

! **ADDITIONAL INFO:** Generally only sushi chefs outside Japan develop sushi items with vegetarians in mind. Not many people in Japan are vegetarian because the food is based on fish, so many of the health concerns arising in other cultures as a result of red meat consumption do not cause people to become vegetarians.

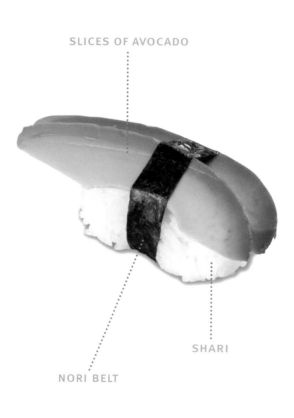

SLICES OF AVOCADO

アボカドニギリ

SHARI

NORI BELT

A chef uses either one large chunk or two or three smaller slices of avocado to make this.

Kaiware-Nigiri *(Radish Sprout Nigiri)*

≈ | **ORIGIN:** *Kaiware daikon* are the sprouts of the daikon radish, and are a very basic and widely used ingredient in sushi, often included in a chef's selection of *nigiri*.

🍙 | **PRESENTATION:** Daikon radish sprouts are white stems with little green leaves at the tips. Usually this sushi item will have a little band of nori wrapped around it to hold it together.

✕ | **TASTE & TEXTURE:** *Kaiwarina* has a crispy crunch from the fresh daikon sprouts, which are lightly flavored and a bit spicy.

🛍 | **PRICE:** $

! | **ADDITIONAL INFO:** *Kaiware* is a great item to order at the very end of a sushi meal, or to have as a cleanser in between pieces of *nigiri* or sashimi. It is also added to a number of rolls such as Spider rolls (see page 146) and vegetarian rolls (see page 180). If you enjoy the spice of *kaiware* you might try asking the chef to include it in another type of roll to add a bit of kick.

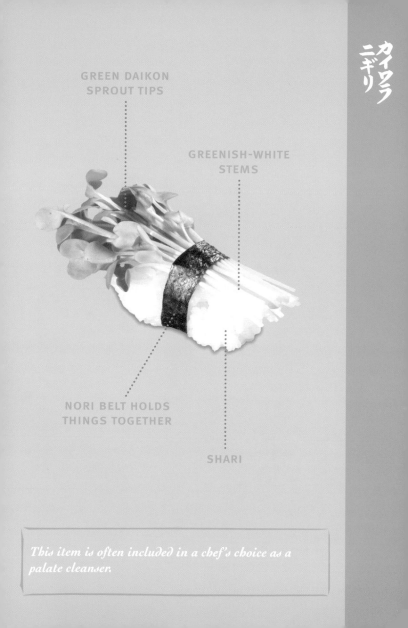

カイワラニギリ

GREEN DAIKON
SPROUT TIPS

GREENISH-WHITE
STEMS

NORI BELT HOLDS
THINGS TOGETHER

SHARI

This item is often included in a chef's choice as a palate cleanser.

Nattō-Maki (Fermented Soybean Roll)

ORIGIN: *Nattō* is a very Japanese item that is made by fermenting soybeans with bacteria. It is packaged and sold widely in food stores in Japan, where it is often eaten over rice or mixed with a raw egg for breakfast. Other popular *nattō* dishes are *nattō miso* soup and *nattō tempura*.

INGREDIENTS: Nori, *shari*, wasabi, scallions, and *nattō*.

PRESENTATION: *Nattō-maki* is served in the *hoso-maki* style, with the light brown-colored *nattō* at the center.

TASTE & TEXTURE: The texture is slimy and the taste is an acquired one. If you're looking for something healthy, this is it, but I would not suggest this to someone who is just starting to eat sushi—*nattō-maki* has the potential to turn them off sushi completely. Often a chef will add sugar to *nattō* to sweeten it and make it easier to eat.

PRICE: $

ADDITIONAL INFO: The bacteria from the fermented soybean is said to be very good for you, so this is an excellent item for vegetarians. When *nattō* ferments, it gives off a very pungent smell. Those who like *nattō* grow to like this smell very much, but it is as off-putting as the flavor to people who don't know *nattō*. If you do develop a taste for it, it is also very good with fish in a roll.

巻ナット

LIGHT BROWN
NATTŌ

SHARI

NORI OUTSIDE

People who like nattō *often ask for it to be added to other rolls.*

Vegetarian Roll

ORIGIN: This roll was created in America with vegetarians in mind.

INGREDIENTS: Vegetarian rolls can contain any variety of fresh or pickled veggies along with nori, *shari,* and wasabi. The ingredients included in the roll pictured here are *kaiware, kampyo,* carrot, *oshinko,* and cucumber.

PRESENTATION: This *ura-maki* looks like a salad rolled in *shari* and nori.

TASTE & TEXTURE: The taste is refreshing and the texture is both crunchy and soft, like a salad with rice.

PRICE: $

ADDITIONAL INFO: This roll is also very nice in the *te-maki* style—like a vegetable ice cream cone!

RADISH SPROUTS

NORI

KAMPYO

CARROT

PICKLED
DAIKON

SESAME
SEEDS

CUCUMBER

SHARI OUTSIDE

Like spider rolls, veggie rolls are served with the ingredients bursting out of the roll, enhancing the appearance.

Other Sushi Dishes

Additional Preparations Commonly Found in a Sushi-Ya

....

In this section are a few traditional sushi preparations, while some of the following items allow the chef to choose the best and freshest ingredients of the day and present them to you. When you're not sure what to order, try a chef's choice plate.

Variety dishes involve a number of different ingredients and garnishes and offer the most visually pleasing sushi experience. The chef will always do his most creative work presenting these. Once you are ready to try anything, order one—you'll appreciate the artistry and variety of sushi at its absolute best.

盛合せ

Hako-Zushi, Oshi-Zushi
(Box Sushi)

ORIGIN: *Hako-zushi* is a style that has come a long way, originating as the first combination of fish and rice eaten together. *Hako-zushi* mimics the old method of preserving fish that the Chinese originated. The *Edomae* style of *nigiri-zushi* was developed from the principles of this preparation.

INGREDIENTS: *Shari* and any kind of fish.

PRESENTATION: *Oshi bako* (press boxes) are used to form this type of sushi. The fish is laid in the bottom of the box, and rice is added over the top of the fish. The chef then puts the lid on and presses it down to compact the fish and rice into a rectangular loaf that is removed and cut into smaller rectangular pieces.

TASTE & TEXTURE: This is the sushi in which you can taste the past. The flavor of the fish with the texture of the pressed rice is solid and pleasant.

PRICE: $$$

ADDITIONAL INFO: It is said that *oshi-zushi* was developed by rice merchants in Osaka, Japan.

はこ寿し

ANY TYPE OF SEAFOOD CAN BE USED;
EBI AND UNAGI ARE PICTURED HERE

SHARI

CUT INTO RECTANGLES

There are usually six pieces in a portion of hako-zushi, *because of the size of the press box.*

Tekka Domburi (*Tuna Bowl*)

≈ | **ORIGIN:** *Tekka domburi* is from the *Edomae* sushi style. This dish is a very popular item in the U. S. as well as Japan.

▽ | **INGREDIENTS:** *Shari,* wasabi, *shiso, tamago,* and *akami.* Other garnishes such as cucumber or shredded nori may also be added.

⌒ | **PRESENTATION:** This dish is a bowl of sushi rice with tuna arranged artistically over the top, and everything else adding color as a garnish. It may appear that the chef has made slices in each of the pieces of fish, but these are just the natural layers that exist in tuna, revealed by the chef through a technique of cutting the meat "against the grain."

✕ | **TASTE & TEXTURE:** This dish is for the tuna lovers. The tuna flavors and textures are the focus.

△ | **PRICE:** $$$

! | **ADDITIONAL INFO:** You can order other *domburi* dishes, with whatever topping you'd like. For instance, *hamachi domburi* is a popular item. You may also see *tekka-hama domburi,* a mixture of tuna and yellowtail.

SHISO
GARNISH

TAMAGO
GARNISH

AKAMI
MAGURO

鉄火丼

SHARI

LINES SHOW THE NATURAL
LAYERS IN THE MEAT

WASABI

A chef will often arrange a piece of fish in a domburi to look like a flower, as you see here.

Chirashi-Zushi
(Assorted Raw Fish over Rice)

≈ **ORIGIN:** This is from the Edo period and is the result of the artistry of one of the Tokyo chefs.

▽ **INGREDIENTS:** Assorted raw fish and *shari,* along with any number of garnishes such as *tamago, shiso,* or *gari.* The ingredients in this particular *chirashi-zushi* are *akami, karei, bincho, madai, ikura, ika, ebi, hokkigai, tako, suzuki, saba, kanpachi,* and *sake.*

⊟ **PRESENTATION:** The concept used by chefs when presenting this dish is to make it appear to be a small garden, with a bouquet of vibrant shapes and colors.

✂ **TASTE & TEXTURE:** This is a great way to explore the many flavors and textures of different fish as if you were conducting a taste test.

△ **PRICE:** $$$-$$$$

! **ADDITIONAL INFO:** *Chirashi* is a dish developed in the Edo period as a derivative of the Kansai-style preparation called *bara-zushi,* in which all the ingredients are cooked and mixed into the sushi rice, like a jumbalaya.

SHISO
GARNISH

TAMAGO
GARNISH

THE FRESHEST FISH
ARE ARRANGED ARTISTICALLY
OVER RICE

ちらし
寿し

WASABI

GINGER AND
SCALLION GARNISH

Chirashi *give the chef an opportunity to show the variety of fish available at the* sushi-ya.

Sashimi Moriawase
(Chef's Choice Sashimi Plate)

ORIGIN: This is another dish that was born out of the creativity of Japanese sushi chefs.

INGREDIENTS: As with other "chef's choice" plates, *sashimi moriawase* includes the freshest fish of the day presented with garnishes such as *shiso* or shredded *kaiware,* as well as wasabi and *gari.* Pictured in this selection are *suzuki, tai, sake, akami, mirugai, kanpachi,* and *saba.*

PRESENTATION: Various types of fish are sliced and arranged with a variety of garnishes, exhibiting a wide variety of colors and shapes. Generally these will come with three or four pieces of each fish used.

TASTE & TEXTURE: As with all of the "chef's choice" dishes, this is a great way to make sure that you are getting the freshest and best fish available.

PRICE: $$$

ADDITIONAL INFO: Often the chef will serve certain pieces of sashimi on *shiso* (perilla leaves). This plant from the mint family has a great flavor, and you will often see these leaves used for sushi. If you do get *shiso* with your *sashimi moriawase,* be sure to try one of the pieces of fish wrapped in a leaf.

盛合せ

THREE TO FOUR SLICES OF THE FRESHEST FISH ARE PRESENTED FOR A VARIETY OF SHAPES AND COLORS

GARI TO CLEANSE THE PALATE

GRATED DAIKON

WASABI

SHISO GARNISH

Shiso *leaves and grated daikon radish are often used to make a sashimi plate resemble a garden.*

Sushi Moriawase
(Chef's Choice Sushi Plate)

≈ | **ORIGIN:** Serving a variety of *nigiri-zushi* arranged together is, again, an old Japanese style of presentation, but local ingredients and creativity ensure that no two *moriawase* are the same.

▽ | **INGREDIENTS:** This particular *sushi moriawase* includes *akami, suzuki, ebi, hotategai, hokkigai, madai, sake, bincho,* and *karei,* along with half of a California roll and half of a *kampyo-maki.*

⊟ | **PRESENTATION:** This assortment of *nigiri-zushi* often comes with one full *maki-mono,* or halves of two types of roll. It will also often include a vegetarian *nigiri* item, or perhaps a piece of *tamago nigiri.*

✕ | **TASTE & TEXTURE:** This is a great dish for people who have not had the chance to try all different types of fish. The textures will vary from mild to chewy, depending on the fish. The tastes are all a little different also.

♙ | **PRICE:** $$$

! | **ADDITIONAL INFO:** It is not uncommon for people who order these dishes to do so as a way to sample what is best at a *sushi-ya* on a given day. Once they are finished, they will order more of what they liked.

SERVED WITH ONE FULL
ROLL OR HALVES OF TWO ROLLS

GARI TO CLEANSE
THE PALATE

WASABI

AN ASSORTMENT OF
THE CHEF'S BEST NIGIRI

In Japan, one sushi moriawase *is traditionally only
eight pieces of* nigiri *and one roll.*

Acknowledgments

I dedicate this book to my mother, Betty Etsuko Suetsugu, who passed in April of 2003. She really loved sushi—the last food she ate was tuna sushi. She was from Kyoto, where she learned to make *saba-zushi*. My first taste of sushi was from the *saba-zushi* she made.

To my father, George Sadao Suetsugu, I would like to say thanks for his love and support, and for providing the Japanese characters you see throughout this book. He is a master calligrapher.

To my brothers and sisters, thanks for the laughter and tears we share in life.

Special thanks to Leighton Armitage for his expertise, educational support, knowledge, and his friendship.

And last of all, thanks to the two people closest to me—my wife, Bing, who gives me all her loving support, and my daughter, Aiko, for being the inspiration of my life.

About the Author

Robert Suetsugu, a former sumo wrestler, studied the time-honored art of sushi in Tokyo under master chef Yoshio Takasaki, and perfected his skills in restaurants in Hokkaido, Japan, New York City, and Seattle. He is the proprietor of Sushiman, a Japanese restaurant he established in 1990 in Issaquah, a suburb of Seattle, Washington. He lives in the Seattle area with his wife and daughter.

Glossary: Definitions and Pronunciations of the Japanese Words Used In This Book

An understanding of the sounds of Japanese vowels is the easy first step to correct pronunciation:

A= ah
I= ee
U= oo
E= eh
O= oh

A

Aji: (ah-jee) horse mackerel

Ajino tataki: (ah-jee-NO tah-tah-KEE) a presentation using aji in which the meat is chopped into small pieces and arranged with ginger and scallions

Akagai: (ah-kah-GUY) red clam; also known as the ark shell

Akami: (ah-kah-MEE) red meat tuna

Ama ebi: (ah-MAH eh-BEE) sweet shrimp

Anago: (ah-nah-GO) sea or conger eel

An-kimo: (ahn-kee-MO) monkfish liver

Avocado-maki: (ah-vo-KAH-do mah-KEE) avocado roll

Awabi: (ah-wah-BEE) shellfish with only the top shell

B

Bafun uni: (bah-FOON oo-NEE) green urchin

Bakagai: (bah-kah-GUY) technical name for aoyagi

Bincho: (been-CHO) albacore tuna

Botan ebi: (bo-TAN eh-BEE) spot prawn, the largest of the shrimp used for *ama ebi*

Buri: (boo-ree) yellowtail over ten pounds

C

Chirashi-zushi: (che-RAH-she) assorted raw fish served over rice

Chu-toro: (choo-TOW-ro) medium tuna

E

Ebi: (eh-BEE) common term for shrimp or prawn

Edomae: (eh-do-MY) sushi style with fresh fish served on rice; also known as Kanto-style

Engawa: (en-gah-WAH) the edge of a flatfish

F

Futo-maki: (foo-TOW-mah-KEE) large sushi roll with a combination of cooked and fresh vegetables and usually a piece of egg

G

Gari: (gah-ree) pickled ginger
Geso: (guess-so) squid tentacles
Gohan: (GO-hon) cooked rice

H

Hako-zushi: (hah-KO zoo-shee) sushi style formed with press boxes, also known as *oshi-zushi*
Hamachi: (hah-mah-CHEE) yellowtail, usually eight to ten pounds
Hikari-mono: (hik-ah-REE-mo-no) smaller fish that have silvery, shiny skin
Himo (HE-mo): thread-like filament that connects a clam's body to its shell
Hirame: (hee-rah-MAY) sole or flounder
Hiramasa: (hee-RAH-mah-SAH) a yellowtail relative fished exclusively in the waters of Japan
Hokkigai: (ho-KEE-guy) surf clam
Hokoku aka ebi: (ho-ko-koo ah-KAH eh-BEE) northern red shrimp
Hon Maguro: (hone mah-goo-RO) bluefin tuna from the Atlantic Ocean
Hoso-maki: (ho-so-mah-KEE) thin roll
Hotategai: (ho-TAH-tay-GUY) scallop

I

Ika: (ee-KAH) squid or cuttlefish
Ikura: (ee-koo-rah) salmon eggs
Inada: (ee-nah-dah) yellowtail less than eight pounds
Inari sushi: (ee-nah-REE soo-shee) sushi using small, deep-fried pouches of tofu cooked in sweet soy sauce
Inari age: (ee-nah-REE ah-GEH) small, deep-fried pouches of tofu cooked in sweet soy sauce

K

Kabayaki: (kah-BAH-yah-KEE) barbecue style
Kai: (ky) general term for shellfish
Kaiware nigiri: (ky-wah-REH nee-gee-REE) radish sprout nigiri
Kajiki maguro: (kah-jee-KEE mah-goo-RO) swordfish
Kampyo-maki: (kamp-YO mah-KEE) gourd roll
Kani: (kah-NEE) crab
Kanpachi: (kan-pah-CHEE) amberjack
Kansai: (kan-SI) western region of Japan, where sushi originated
Kanto: (kan-TOW) eastern region of Japan, the common style of sushi
Kappa-maki: (kah-PAH-mah-KEE) cucumber roll
Karei: (kah-REH-ee) the general term for a flatfish with eyes on the right side of its head
Katsuo: (kat-SOO-o) bonito, a red meat fish related to tuna and mackerel
Katsu bushi (cot-sue boo-she): bonito flakes
Kasugo: (kah-SOO-go) young sea bream
Kazunoko: (kah-ZOO-no-KO) herring roe
Kihada maguro: (kee-HA-dah mah-goo-RO) yellowfin tuna
Kodai: (ko-die) baby snapper
Kohada: (ko-hah-DAH) gizzard shad

Kome: (ko-MAY) uncooked short grain rice
Komochi konbu: (ko-muh-chee kon-boo) herring eggs on kelp
Komochi wakame: (ko-muh-chee wah-kah-may) herring eggs on seaweed
Kuro maguro: (koo-ro mah-goo-ro) bluefin tuna from the Pacific Ocean
Kuruma ebi: (koo-roo-MAH eh-BEE) wheel shrimp or prawns
Kyu bon: (cue-BAHN) octopus tentacles

M

Madai: (mah-DIE) red sea bream, also called red snapper
Maguro: (mah-goo-RO) tuna
Maki-mono: (mah-KEE-mo-NO) rolled sushi
Masago: (mah-sah-go) smelt eggs
Matsubagani: (mat-soo-BAH-gah-nee) snow crab also known as zuwai gani
Mebachi Maguro: (meh-bah-CHEE mah-goo-RO) bigeye tuna
Minami Maguro: (mee-nah-MEE mah-goo-RO) southern tuna
Mirugai: (mee-roo-GUY) some of the largest clams used for sushi, including
    geoduck, horse neck clam, and giant clam
Murasaki uni: (moo-RAH-sah-KEE oo-nee) purple urchin

N

Nabe: (nah-BAY) hot pots
Natto-maki: (nah-tow-mah-kee) fermented soybean roll
Negi Hama-maki: (neh-GEE hah-MAH-mah-KEE) yellowtail with scallion roll
Nigiri-zushi: (nee-gee-REE zoo-SHE) hand-formed sushi
Nimono neta: (nee-mo-NO neh-TAH) a cooked item
Nori: (no-REE) dried seaweed

O

Oboro (oh-BOH-ro) fish powder
Odori ebi: (o-do-REE eh-BEE) kuruma ebi served alive, also known as
    "dancing shrimp"
Oshinko-maki: (o-SHEEN-ko-mah-KEE) pickle roll
Oshi bako (oh-SHE BAH-koh) press box
Otoro: (o-TOW-RO) very fatty tuna

R

Rayu: (rah-YOO) a type of chile oil

S

Sake: (sah-keh) salmon
Sake-maki: (sah-keh-mah-kee) salmon roll
Sashimi: (sah-shee-MEE) sliced raw fish or other seafood
Sashimi moriawase: (sah-shee-MEE mo-ree-AH-wah-SEH) chef's choice
    sashimi plate
Shakko: (shah-ko) mantis shrimp

Shima aji: (shee-MAH ah-jee) yellow jack fish, from the yellowtail family
Shime saba: (shee-meh sah-bah) pickled mackerel
Shiromi: (shee-ro-MEE) white meat fish, low in fat and light tasting
Shiso: (shee-so) perilla leaves
Shōyu: (sho-YOO) soy sauce
Su: (soo) rice vinegar
Sunomono: (soo-no-mo-no) salad with a vinaigrette sauce
Sushi moriawase: (soo-shee mo-ree-AH-wah-SEH) chef's choice sushi plate
Suzuki: (soo-zoo-KEE) sea bass

T

Tairagai: (tie-rah-GUY) razor clam
Tako: (tah-ko) octopus
Tamago: (tah-mah-go) sushi omelet made from chicken eggs
Taraba gani: (tah-rah-BAH gah-NEE) king crab
Tarako: (tah-rah-KO) eggs from cod or pollock
Tekka domburi: (teh-kah dom-boo-ree) tuna bowl
Tekka-maki: (teh-kah-mah-KEE) tuna roll
Te-maki: (teh-mah-KEE) hand-rolled sushi
Temp-kasu: (temp-kah-SOO) tempura crumbs
Tobikko: (tow-bee-KO) flying fish eggs, also known as tobiuo-noko
Tobiuo: (tow-BEE-yoo-O) flying fish
Torigai: (tow-ree-GUY) cockle clam
Toro: (tow-RO) fatty tuna

U

Ubagai: (oo-bah-guy) formal name for hokkigai
Uchikawa (oo-chi-KAH-wah): The often shiny layer just beneath the skin of fish
Ume-shiso-maki: (oo-MEH-shee-SO-mah-KEE) sour plum paste with beefsteak
    leaf roll
Unagi: (oo-nah-GEE) freshwater eel
Una-kyu-maki: (oo-nah-CUE-mah-KEE) eel-and-cucumber roll
Uni: (oo-nee) sea urchin
Ura-maki: (oo-RAH-mah-KEE) style of sushi roll in which a half-sheet of nori is
    on the inside of the roll between the fish and other ingredients

W

Wasabi: (wah-SAH-BEE) Japanese horseradish

Y

Yokozuna-maki: (yo-ko-ZOO-nah-mah-KEE) grand champion roll

Z

Zuke: (zoo-KAY) fish
Zuwai gani: (zoo-WAH-ee gah-NEE) snow crab, also known as matsubagai

Index (Japanese and English)